The Faithful Majority
Common Sense Re-Revisited

A Call for Unity and Collaborative Participation

By All Americans to Reignite the American Spirit

I0412000

Alan W. Goldsberry

Alan W. Goldsberry

ISBN: 148483996X
ISBN-13: 978-1484839966

Alan W. Goldsberry

Common Sense *Revisited* (1995)

This book was first released in an abridged version in 1995, as an adaptation and revision of *Common Sense* by Thomas Paine (1776). The objective was to present the similarities of the times and events of 1776 and 1995, along with the call for the People to arise once again and declare their independence and rights to life, liberty and the pursuit of happiness.

Published in an abridged version by Liberty Development, Inc in 1995.

Alan W. Goldsberry

The Faithful Majority: Common Sense *Re-Revisited*

Now released in its full version and updated from 1995 with new essays, quotes and Footnotes from 2012. The times and events of today remain amazingly similar to 1776 and 1995; from the acceleration of technological advances and rapid expansion of mass communications to the need for once again to make the call to reclaim our self-governing rights as Americans. The call for vigilance, unity and collaborative participation by the People is as important today, as in 1776.

This call is being spoken loudly by many more in 2012 than in 1995. The question is, "will it be enough to defeat Politics As Usual, special interests and leaderless, entrenched elected officials? America has been here before and the People have always awakened. The time is now for the *American Spirit* to be fully re-ignited and may the flame of liberty continue to burn for all eternity.

Alan W. Goldsberry

CONTENTS

Alan W. Goldsberry

Alan W. Goldsberry

ACKNOWLEDGMENTS

All my love and thanks to my family and friends for listening and encouraging me all these years.

Alan W. Goldsberry

Overview of this Book

This book is a collection of three books and quotes to emphasize how *We the People* are the best guardians and preservers of freedom, not the politicians or selected privileged few. With this comes the responsibility and accountability, which America's Founders truly believed the People would always stand up when called to fulfill this duty to bring forth our unique *American Spirit* that has led the world to know and experience freedom.

Throughout the writings of America's Founders, they express their beliefs and faith in the general populace to have reason and common sense to oversee human affairs. They understood how the Natural law of society, the will of the majority, would ultimately be the best judge relative to the rights of the people. America's government is structured upon these beliefs and thus designed for its elected and appointed leaders to answer to the general reason of society. They understood there is a need for limited government, yet its leaders must be accountable to the People. These beliefs are also predicated upon the fact that individuals within society understand the responsibility of self-government and remain vigilant to the forces of tyranny and factions that can divide, conquer and enslave society.

Thomas Jefferson wrote in a letter, *"I am not among those who fear the people. They, and not the rich, are our dependence for continued freedom."* In a separate letter to James Madison, Jefferson wrote related to the Constitutional Convention:

> *"After all, it is my principle that the will of the majority should always prevail. If they approve of the proposed Convention in all its parts, I shall concur in it cheerfully, in hopes they will amend it whenever they shall find it work wrong… Above all things I hope the education of the common people will be attended to; convinced that on their good sense we rely with the most security for the preservation of a due degree of liberty."*

It is the Author's hope for the readers to be inspired by some part or aspect of this collection of writings and quotes, which have been merged into this one book. The foundation for these writings comes from the original *Common Sense* by Thomas Paine, published in 1776. In 1995, the Author wrote *Common Sense Revisited*, which was an adaptation of Paine's work to modern day language and current political events. In 2011, the Author revisited his writings and began writing to re-introduce *Common Sense Revisited* with additional observations based upon current political events in 2012.Thus, the new title *The Faithful Majority – Common Sense Re-Revisited*.

The book has six parts. Each part can stand alone. Yet, together a progression reveals how factions and special interests can easily divide the People when selfish interests are chosen over reason and common sense. While factions or special interests will always exist, it is when common people, as Jefferson thus refers, become apathetic because of their frustrations at the special interests and lack of authentic leadership for too long. It is when the common people choose not to *attend to* their responsibility that liberty is its most vulnerable and all benefits of this great nation, America, are put at risk.

Part One is a blend of the original overview to *Common Sense Revisited* (1995) and new writings from 2012. The dates of new writings will be put in parenthesis. Dating the writings is important for the reader to gain perspective that no matter the date, whether 1776, 1995 or 2012, any individual put into a role of power can be corrupted and set aside their duty to the People and become selfish and self-serving or enslaved by the powerful special interests and career legislators. The Founders clearly understood this aspect of human nature. This became ever clearer to the Author, as he reviewed his writings from 1995 and realized the ongoing nature of special interest politics and lack of genuine, authentic political leaders which have now placed America into a more precarious position than in 1995. It is now time for the common people to rise up, not just for the Presidential election of 2012, but to become a force that all politicians know they must answer to and fulfill their duty by becoming the authentic leaders that has made America great.

Part Two contains the Author's original commentary, written in 1995, on his thoughts, philosophy, readings and understanding of *life, liberty and the pursuit of happiness*, rooted in his education, knowledge, observations and experience as it relates to *Common Sense* by Thomas Paine (1776). This collection of essays provides a more specific view on the state of affairs in America in 1995, and was intentionally written to follow closely to Thomas Paine's original writings in 1776. Footnotes written in 2012 are included.

Part Three is the adapted and revised version of *Common Sense* by Thomas Paine (1776), written in 1995 with Footnotes from 2012.

Parts Four and Five are an additional collection of essays from *Common Sense Revisited* (1995), which provide a more specific view on the state of affairs in America (1995) and follows closely to the Thomas Paine's original writings in 1776.

Part Six is a collection of quotes, from 1995 and 2012, to emphasize various concepts throughout the book from other historic and modern day individuals as they relate to past and current trends and conditions regarding society and government.

My message is no secret and it will often appear to repeat itself. The reward for me has been the joy of seeing the words come together with feeling and meaning. One part or one passage may touch the reader, while other parts may not. Some may agree with parts and disagree with others. No matter your thoughts about these writings, my hope is you will take-on a personal effort to discover the *whole ground of history* as it relates to you and your situation and come to appreciate the magnitude and divine providence of the people and events responsible for the founding of America. If some part of my writing forwards you personally to pursue the knowledge to know for yourself more deeply and what it means to be an American versus listening to the media pundits who pander to and parrot the sound-bites of special interests and politicians, I say "good for you." No matter your political persuasion, religion, race or creed, may you strive to become a better person and be the best you can be to serve and contribute to the lives of others, to America and the world. Then this country will definitely continue to move forward as the greatest nation on earth and influence all nations to strive for *life, liberty and the pursuit of happiness.*

Prologue for Common Sense *Re-Revisited*
(August 2012)

This Prologue was written to capture a few of my thoughts (the Author) as I re-read my original writings of 1995. The book is separated into six Parts. All Footnotes have two purposes. (1) They contain additional reflections, thoughts and personal commentary based upon current day, 2012; or (2) they are quotes to further emphasize or illustrate a concept or point.

Common Sense Revisited was originally set to be self-published in the second quarter of 1995. An abridged version was published for pre-launch promotions and a website was developed, which received national recognition through USA Today Top Ten Websites and other publication mentions.

As the Author, I had promoted the upcoming book on some forty radio talk shows from mid-1994 until April 19, 1995, the date of the Oklahoma City bombing of the federal building by Timothy McVeigh. Two radio shows were booked that morning. Both were cancelled and no additional guest appearances were pursued to discuss the book and marketing efforts stopped. It did not seem appropriate in the midst of such tragic loss of life by the hands of extreme right-wing terrorism.

I was shocked, saddened, angry and prayerful, like the rest of the nation, as the days and weeks unfolded. Stories were told of the peoples' lives that died and injured, along with the heroics and the immediate outpouring of aid and volunteers from all across the nation and world. The contrast of people often viewed as common everyday type folks becoming uncommon in every respect.

It was clear the *Faithful Majority* was alive and well. You will learn more about the *Faithful Majority* in the book. Suffice it to say, the *Faithful Majority* are the people you associate with every day, at work, in the community, school, church and various life activities. Each member of the *Faithful Majority* is unique, with very different experiences, knowledge, education and opinions. They come from all walks of life, different races, generations, religions and financial status; and when push comes to shove and an event such as an extremist attack, we can always count on the *Faithful Majority* to step forth and do what's right for others in need – to extend a helping hand. The *Faithful Majority* are the common folks who never cower or fade in times of need and sacrifice. They stand tall and do what it takes because it is their heritage and birthright as an American. It is in their DNA to stand tall and give all they can, including their mind, heart, soul and even their life.

The Oklahoma City bombing brought forth the reality of how words of common sense and reason can be easily perverted into such extremist actions, costing the lives of innocent individuals who simply were living out another day in their lives with family, work and community. Sadly, terrorism struck again six years later on 9/11/01, and this time from foreign terrorists.

These acts of terrorism are wrong and cannot be allowed to become the way of this world. Nor can we allow politicians in America and throughout the world to deny their call of duty to represent the People they serve. If the politicians continue with their endless, blaming rhetoric and stalemates (kicking the can down the road), they will weaken all nations. In such events, the People always rise up against the obvious lack of political leadership. The question becomes, which People will rise up? History has proven weak, selfish, power-hungry leaders open the door for extreme fundamental terrorists to prey upon the disadvantaged and outcast. They deliver a message of victimization by the rich and create class warfare rhetoric. We all know (or should know) the results of such extreme fundamentalists beliefs and actions against anyone of wealth, any race or religious belief different than theirs. We think we are beyond such times, yet consider North Korea, other such countries ruled by tyrants and the recent May 2012, Greek elections, when fed-up Greek voters turned to both the extreme-left and extreme-right, a Communist Party and a Neo-Nazi Party.

Amazing how in just a couple of generations removed from the human tragedies of Hitler that such belief could be rising up again. While, it may be in doubt of such an outcome becoming reality in American elections, vigilance must be like a lighthouse beacon as a warning of those rocky shores. It is clear that current political events and gyrations during the Great

Recession of 2008 demonstrate how easily weak and selfish political leadership fragment voters.

Fragmented voters turn to the passionate orator who blames and ridicules instead of presenting a plan of action, because the passionate orator knows no plan is needed when blaming others can win the election. When the orator arrives to their elected position without a plan, they have no sense of duty to the People; they are drunk with desire for the power more than fulfilling their representative duty to the Nation. They are inexperienced with untested character to stand in the arena with the cunning temptations of power. A powerful speaker does not equate to being a powerful leader. Often, just the opposite is true. In time, they are proven to be incapable of doing what's right and their failures of leadership become clear. Yet, they continue to speak more loudly with blame and division. And, thus the lighthouse beacon, thought to be of no use anymore, now burns brightly for the *Faithful Majority* to awaken and do what needs to be done to make America strong and vibrant, again – for all Americans, not the chosen few of the passionate orator.

The desire to life, liberty and the pursuit of happiness is a desire of humanity, not just for Americans. It must be preserved and allowed to thrive. Thomas Paine wrote of the danger in allowing ourselves to begin to think it continues to be okay with the leaderless ways elected officials are managing these current times. The danger to consider is that as time continues to move forward without meaningful change in the course and direction of *Politics As Usual*, the passage of time favors the fundamentalists. It is definitely time for *Common Sense* to be re-revisited again.

> *"A long habit of not thinking a thing wrong, gives it a superficial appearance of being right, and raises at first a formidable outcry in defense of custom. But the tumult soon subsides. Time makes more converts than reason."* ~ Thomas Paine ~

Now, as I bring *Common Sense Re-Revisited* to publication, it is abundantly clear these rapidly changing, complex and chaotic times, while creating turmoil for many, it is clearly creating expansive opportunities, equally to all. The *tumult* of 1994 subsided and *time* has clearly made more *converts than reason* of self-serving politicians. They have used the turmoil and crisis to expand their influence and power, when they could have done what's right. In contrast, private citizens and businesses will use the same turmoil and crisis to restructure and re-tool and be faithful for the coming times of future growth. But, this is not a passive faith. Already, the Faithful Majority have decided a change must be made.

Just as the Founding Fathers declared their independence, so do the Faithful Majority. They know victory is for the taking. Already, they are asking, seeking and finding abundant opportunities to expand by leveraging the Internet and technology with creative and cost effective solutions to very complicated issues that impact the daily human condition. They are doing this even when America and the world have endured additional terrorists' actions, wars, epidemic scares and severe economic crisis. Many are to blame for the current times. Yet, only the selfish, self-centered politicians and people who see themselves as victims continue to blame others. In contrast, the *Faithful Majority* embraces self-reliance and takes personal responsibility for their lives and situations. These are the people who are building the future and making a difference by building a stronger, better future for themselves, family and community by modeling the way for others. They are not waiting for the passionate orator to build it for them. They realize the experiment with the passionate orator has failed and it is time to make things right, once again.

Take a moment to consider the immense possibilities for America and humanity if we heed these words of Theodore Roosevelt within a sense of unity and collaborative participation to create new possibilities for ALL People.

"I am a strong individualist by personal habit, inheritance, and conviction; but it is a mere matter of common sense to recognize that the State, the community, the citizens acting together, can do a number of things better than if they were left to individual action."

We stand not at the edge of some fiscal cliff, as many media and weak politicians want us to believe. In reality, we stand at the summit with the next higher summit in clear view. We must throw out all weak politicians who would stand in the way of this grand new adventure of a world thriving on creating solutions that achieve the hopes and dreams which have existed since the dawn of humanity. Leave the self-serving politicians to their emptiness and obsessive natures for power like Gollum, the fictional character in J.R.R. Tolkien's *Lord of the Rings*. These Gollum-like politicians continually lust for the power yet only desire it if they can be free of personal liability. Of course, they want to be free of what doesn't work because they don't take ownership of their responsibility for poor and failed outcomes.

Likewise, much is being said and done today in 2012 that sounds very similar to 1995. Our differences and special interests continue to divide us, not for the lack of common sense and reason, but more so out of frustration with the lack of leadership's ability to determine the common ground for the common good versus the highest paying special interest. We only need to turn toward the brightly shining lighthouse beacon and be mindful of just how close America is coming to those rocky shores of liberty lost; where future generations' wonder why we would let such liberties and freedoms slip through our fingers. The following appeared on the inside cover of the original *Common Sense Revisited* in 1995.

> *Many words have been written and spoken about humanity's passion for freedom and liberty. Many actions have been taken; many lives have suffered and died for millions to have their right to embrace the blessings of freedom and liberty.*
>
> *Differences at their worst have divided families and led to wars. In the worst of times, an unlikely individual recognizes the desires of the People and stands as their leader. People are inspired to conquer their fears and do what must be done to make it the way it should be.*
>
> *Will one stand for America before the worst of times? Will the people listen and take action? When will we choose to declare ourselves? When will we make life in America the way it should be?*

As I re-read my writings, I found myself coming full circle and back to the writings of Thomas Paine and the Founding Fathers. I began to think more about the writers, themselves, than just their words – and how their knowledge, experiences and *the times they lived in,* influenced their personal faith, beliefs and values. Then, in combination with the recorded history of the results of their decisions and actions, I got a glimpse into the core of their character. It is clear from their extensive writings that their associations both encouraged and challenged each to think differently, clearly and extensively of their decisions and how those decisions would impact multiple future generations. I have reconciled, for myself, the immense impact of their lives and how the results of their actions bless me and all of us with abundant opportunities to stand upon their shoulders and the shoulders of our immediate *Greatest Generation* to create an even greater nation and world.

One of the important impacts upon me was realizing the men and women during the Revolutionary period wrote about how they genuinely considered the impact of their actions upon future generations, not just solely focused on personal self-interests. This can be seen by the an entry made by George Washington into his journal, as he leaves Mount Vernon to be sworn in as the first President of the United States of America and also by a remark Martha Washington made to her nephew.

> *"About ten o'clock, I bade adieu to Mount Vernon, to private life, and to domestic felicity and, with a mind oppressed with more anxious and painful sensations than I have words to express, set out for New York...with the best dispositions to render service to my country in obedience to its call, but with less hope of answering its expectations."*

> Martha comments to her nephew, *"I think it was much too late for him to go into public life again, but it was not to be avoided. Our family will be deranged as I must soon follow him."*

I've come to identify this as a distinctive thinking style of successful people and leaders who have gained the respect from others and willingly embraced the full responsibility of their influence and actions; while cloaked in a quiet passionate sense of duty and call into destiny with an endearing compassion for others. This thinking style, steeped in a character of distinction, which I call *Both/And* thinking empowers these individuals to *think through* situations by embracing two or more thoughts at the same time.

Washington used *Both/And* thinking as he reconciled his desires for a private, quiet life at Mount Vernon and the call of a new nation in need of authentic leadership. People such as Washington developed the ability for skillful thinking which allowed them to hold multiple thoughts at the same time, be active listeners and observers, make clear distinctions of various issues and differences of opinion, and then make decisions that leverage available resources to make significant impacts on the lives of others. One must remember when reading the writings of the Founding Fathers, they wrote with quill pens. Scratch outs are very rare and they obviously had time to think in between dips of the quill.

For me, now in 2012, with an additional twenty more years of life experiences, continual reading and the design and publishing of a personal framework for thinking, I realize how much I learned from these great thinkers and many other mentors how to *think through* complex situations and seek out alternative solutions and new possibilities. In 2011, I once again tuned my listening to the political rhetoric as a few friends inquired about *Common Sense Revisited* and encouraged me to bring it back for publishing. So, I dusted off the files and began to consider publishing *Common Sense Re-Revisited*. I've added the additional "Re" to Revisited because it is the second time to be publishing *Common Sense Revisited*. It is now seventeen years later and twenty years from the time I began writing *Common Sense Revisited*, during the Presidential Elections of 1992.

As I read through *Common Sense Revisited*, I could not be overly surprised at the similarities of the times of 1994 and 2012 relative to the political rhetoric and *Politics As Usual*. It was 1990 when I first recognized how the words of Thomas Paine's *Common Sense* could be adapted and updated to 1994 in order to express similar thoughts and feelings that existed in the colonists of 1775. The desire for alternatives to any current status quo is as old as humanity, especially in the midst of weak or tyrannical leadership. The uniqueness of *Common Sense*, which called forth the *American Spirit* to pursue and endure the American Revolution and the formation of the United States government, demonstrated a new alterative in which to lay the groundwork for achieving life, liberty and the pursuit of happiness.

Obviously, my writings and the current national political discourse is neither new nor original. It's all been written and spoken before. So, why would I throw my writings into the fray if it's just a regurgitation of past historical writings and the vast amount of current day discourse? Interestingly, regurgitation is defined as repeating what has been read or taught, in a way that produces little evidence of genuine personal thought or understanding. *"If we don't read and understand history, we are bound to repeat it"* or a similar quote is often repeated when it is clear the current times are simply repeating what's been done in the past. This is not a regurgitation, but a thoughtful reflection on our times and future.

From my perspective, after listening to the current day political rhetoric and armed with my deep understandings of the character and intent of the Founding Fathers, I find that little evidence exists of genuine personal thought and understanding around the reality of *Politics As Usual*. To clarify, I'm referring to politicians - not so much the *Faithful Majority* because there is some evidence of genuine personal thought and understanding in a broader expanse of the people – and, there needs to be more. To support my reasoning in just one instance – it is clear politicians have not put forth genuine personal thought and understanding because the Federal deficits and debts have tripled since 1994. This is exactly in the opposite direction from the ongoing politicians' promises, contracts and commitments of both political parties over the last eighteen years. The necessary changes must come from within the *Faithful Majority* and selected politicians who choose to be representatives of the People and become the authentic leaders their duty and service to the People demand. In consideration of these reasons and many others, here is a selected few purposes as to why I decided to publish *Common Sense Re-Revisited*:

- A new generation of voters, including my two sons, might be encouraged to read and understand for themselves that *Politics As Usual* with some historical perspective versus just the current-day, empty-promises rhetoric.

- Some of the older generations have yet to take time to read and understand these same issues. They have been raised on and become addicted to a diet of sound-bites and advertising to influence their votes. Likewise, they should be encouraged to read and seek understanding through thoughtful discourse with others versus getting frustrated and parroting sound-bites declarations designed to manipulate thinking.[1]

- The older generations must decide to be responsible for the issues at hand and choose to leave a sustainable legacy for our progeny versus forcing future generations to deal with the issues we could not. Now is the time for older generations to be the authentic leaders or be despised by their grandchildren and beyond.

- It is most concerning to think politicians today may not have taken time to study and understand history. It is clear politicians today either do not know history or they choose to ignore it and pursue personal selfish interests in the midst of the *Faithful Majority* being apathetic and uninvolved. This is the reality of *Politics As Usual*. Those who know the system best know how to game the system to their advantage and ideologies. How can we stand for such blatant abuse, fraud and waste as such politicians reward themselves at the peoples' expense?

From re-reading my writings from 1995, it has become ever clearer why we refer to the men involved in the creation of American government, as Founders of the United States. Likewise, individuals who are willing to take the risks to create and bring forth a new business, they are referred to as founders. If you listen to a founder of any successful, sustainable organization, you will hear their depth of understanding of all aspects of the business. They have studied, researched, read all they can get their hands on, spent extensive amounts of time thinking and dreaming and been engaged in hundreds of discussions – and when the defining moment arrived for them to bring forth their concept, they were prepared and willing to be continually learning, in the midst of all the forward movement and activity.

---

1   From George Washington's Farewell Address: *The Spirit of Party...exists under different shapes in all governments ...but, in those of the popular form, it is seen in its greatest rankness, and is truly their worst enemy. The alternate domination of one faction over another, sharpened by the spirit of revenge, natural to party dissension ...is itself a frightful despotism. It serves always to distract the public councils and enfeeble the public administration. It agitates the community with ill-founded jealousies and false alarms, kindles the animosity of one part against another.*

Now, take a moment to imagine just how much time in reading, writing and discussions the Founders of the United States engaged – and remember, they did not have the distractions or the tools available to founders today. I believe any person who desires to run for any political office should be required to take a history course and engage with others in discourse over the process that the Founders of the United States traversed to bring forth this great nation. This is not a course of study designed from a political perspective – it is designed around the writings and quotes of the Founders. It could only be from individuals who had deep, deep understanding into nature, human nature and the history of failures of representative government. Yet, in the midst of their knowledge, character and leadership something existed that gave them the faith they could make self-government work when it had never worked before. How many founders of organizations do we recognize today? How many individuals have brought forth a new creation that benefits all of society?

This is why I am re-revisiting Common Sense. It is imperative for the Faithful Majority to read, understand and appreciate from where their thoughts, motivations, spirit and faith for the designs of the American government and, more so, their dreams and desire to experience life, liberty and the pursuit of happiness, brought forth into reality by groups of people (men and women) from two hundred and forty years ago. To create any concept that survives, grows and thrives over that period of time has something worth believing in and learning to know for oneself, not what some other person with a design upon their self-interest, wants you to believe.

In Parts Two and Three of the book, the reader will find references to the times and events of the early 1990s. Interestingly, there are great similarities and predictions of future possibilities because of the design of the American government/political process and, obviously, due to the *American Spirit* and foresight by James Madison (Father of the Constitution and fourth President).[2]

---

2   James Madison: *Among the numerous advantages promised by a well-constructed Union, none deserves to be more accurately developed than its tendency to break and control the violence of faction. The friend of popular governments never finds himself so much alarmed for their character and fate, as when he contemplates their propensity to this dangerous vice…The instability, injustice, and confusion introduced into the public councils, have, in truth, been the mortal diseases under which popular governments have everywhere perished.*

The passage of time reminds us those who fail to learn history are fated to repeat it. Another thought to this is those who know history can manipulate others with tweets and sound-bites engaging undisciplined minds to become enraged and say things they know nothing about.

We clearly live in different times than Thomas Paine, George Washington and others from their time. Yet, I assert that they would wholeheartedly agree with this response Albert Einstein writes in a 1946 New York Times magazine:

> *Many persons have inquired concerning a recent message of mine that "a new type of thinking is essential if mankind is to survive and move to higher levels." Often in evolutionary processes a species must adapt to new conditions in order to survive. Today the atomic bomb has altered profoundly the nature of the world as we know it, and the human race consequently finds itself in a new habitat to which it must adapt its thinking. In light of new knowledge...an eventual world state is not just desirable in the name of brotherhood, it is necessary for survival... Today we must abandon competition and secure cooperation. This must be the central fact in all our considerations of international affairs; otherwise we face certain disaster. Past thinking and methods did not prevent world wars. Future thinking must prevent wars.*

I encourage you to take on a new thinking style. Embrace *Both/And* thinking and consider two or more thoughts at the same time and *think through* all the opinions and differences in people to create new alternatives and possibilities that secure unity and collaborative participation. Also, you will read later how Benjamin Franklin made an emotional call to prayer during the Constitutional Convention in 1787. When one considers the multitude of factions and special interests then and now, evoking a higher power, a divine providence, may just be the only way everyone comes to their common sense and has the ability to reason what is the best way to move forward. Apparently, it worked in 1787. Thank You, God and Benjamin Franklin.

Why Re-Revisit Thomas Paine's Common Sense in the Year 2012?

Common Sense by Thomas Paine was published in January 1776. This pamphlet was recognized, at the time and even today, two hundred and forty years later, as an immensely influential writing that inspired the colonists and leaders to seek independence from England. His use of plain language spoke clearly to the common people of the American colonies.

In 1990, I found myself inspired by Paine's simple, yet amazingly thoughtful writing that so easily revealed the reality of the current situation between England and the colonies. And then, he presented a vision for the America to come, which released an awakening in the American colonists that still reverberates throughout the world. *Common Sense* became the orchestra leader of a chorus of the common people singing loudly and in harmony for the opportunity to achieve self-government cloaked in common sense. The seeds of independence had been brewing for decades prior to 1776, but the wide distribution of *Common Sense* throughout all the colonies was the lightening rod that ignited people into action, resulting in a greatness that cannot be denied. Even the span of time nor the factions of political correctness have been able to re-write history when the actual writings of America's Founders have been preserved in books, institutions and easily distributed all throughout the Internet.

As I continued reading and researching Paine's *Common Sense* a seed of thought was planted with me to ponder on how a little adaptation and updating of the words and concepts presented by Paine could be as relevant for today's modern reader of the 20th and now, 21st centuries. The more I pursued this thought, the more Paine's *Common Sense* became as relevant to me as it did for the colonists and leaders of 1776 colonial America. It became the inspiration for me to read more and seek out a deep understanding as to the thoughts, motivations, ambitions and actions of America's Founders.

In the midst of my studies, along came the Presidential elections of 1992 and subsequently the Congressional elections of 1994. Multiple factions of special interests were evolving into political machines threatening all common sense – all for personal gain and clearly predicted by warnings from the Founders. I was continually amazed at how the writings of Paine and many others from those founding times made them vibrantly relevant and alive in current times. I've often felt like I was in the movie *Bill and Ted's Excellent Adventure* – going back and forth in time to have conversations with the Founding Fathers.

By all appearances, especially for an individual who has read or studied only the minimal of American history, the current times could be viewed as very different and not at all relevant to the times of two hundred and forty years ago. Yet, even in a two hundred year span of time, society and people are still relatively the same when it comes to basic human needs especially the ambitions and desire for freedom and the opportunity to life, liberty and pursuit of happiness.

I imagine the Founding Fathers would be intrigued by the industrial and technological advances and not at all surprised by the sameness of human nature. And, I believe they would be pleased by how their design of government has endured and how they knew a leader's true character and ambitions would be easily revealed when in a position of power over the common people. Lastly, based upon their writings and other historical documents, it appears they would be concerned by the rapid expansion of government and how many people are forced to endure the policies and regulations created by incapable politicians and bureaucracies today. America's Founders might even be tempted to say, *"We told you to be aware of these things. When will the common people arise again?"*

In *Common Sense (1776)*, Paine captured basic truths and popular beliefs while connecting those to the ideas of independence and a design of government that brought forth a new, distinctive political identity. This new identity had only been a theoretical concept in the writings and discussions of many scholars and writers over hundreds of years. Yet, Paine's written words empowered hundreds of thousands of colonists to not only consider the possibilities of this new identity, but they came to believe it attainable. It was a fascinating time in 1776, not unlike the early days of the Internet. There was an explosion of communication through printed pamphlets and newspapers and letters were delivered throughout the world. A vibrant discourse on independence erupted throughout the colonies as more than 500,000 copies of *Common Sense* were printed and distributed to a population estimated to be 2.5 million. 20% of the population had a pamphlet, which means total readership could have extended to 30 or 40% of the population. This would be equivalent to a book today selling 15 to 30 million copies in just a few months.

Obviously with a groundswell of this sort, it is easy to understand why individuals of proven character and leadership became compelled to embrace the concepts and ideas with a deep sense of meaning and purpose; many felt it became more of a calling than a duty. George Washington wrote to Thomas Jefferson, *"I find Common Sense is working a powerful change in the minds of many men."* And, John Adams wrote, *"Without the pen of the author of Common Sense, the sword of Washington would have been raised in vain."* It is important to realize the publication and distribution of *Common Sense* began in January 1776 and the Declaration of Independence was drafted, edited, put through debate, adopted, written and signed by fifty six people on July 4, 1776. This happened in just six months during times when communications took days to weeks to have letters delivered. Instant communications is available today – and, how long does it take for politicians to get anything done, today?

Paine's common sense message, for many, became as much a sense of destiny as it was a duty to God and Country. They sacrificed everything for the opportunity to bring forth something never achieved before, which, today, we recognize as the American Spirit. In reality and proven throughout history, the founding of America became their legacy to birth a nation of such grand ideals and magnitude that the ambitions of our Founding Fathers and Mothers have yet to be achieved.

It is with these understandings and a sense of calling, for me, that I share my years of reading, research and writing. It is my hope it will inspire you to pursue for yourself, gain new knowledge, acquire deep understanding and gain a more vibrant appreciation for that quiet, ever-present *Spirit* that resides deep within this nation and continues to call America and its People to greatness.

August 2012

Alan W. Goldsberry, Husband, Father, Friend, Entrepreneur, Author

Member of the Faithful Majority

Diary of a Legislative Body

~ Will Rogers ~

From the "Leaves of Gold" published in 1948

Monday - Soak the rich.

Tuesday - Begin hearing from the rich.

Tuesday Afternoon - Decide to give the rich a chance to get richer.

Wednesday - Tax Wall Street stock sales.

Thursday - Get word from Wall Street: "Lay off us or you will get no campaign contributions."

Thursday Afternoon - Decide: "We are wrong about Wall Street."

Friday - Soak the little fellow.

Saturday Morning - Find out there is no little fellow. He has been soaked until he is drown.

Sunday - Meditate.

Next Week - Same procedure, only more talk and less results.

Excerpts from History by Ralph Waldo Emerson

There is one mind common to all individual men. Every man is an inlet to the same and to all of the same. He that is once admitted to the right of reason is made a freeman of the whole estate. What Plato has thought, he may think; what a saint has felt, he may feel; what at any time has befallen any man, he can understand. Who hath access to this universal mind is a party to all that is or can be done, for this is the only and sovereign agent.

We sympathize in the great moments of history, in the great discoveries, the great resistances, the great prosperities of men; because there law was enacted, the sea was searched, the land was found, or the blow was struck, for us, as we ourselves in that place would have done or applauded.

PART ONE

Introduction

For All Children – Author Dedication and Acknowledgments

This Begins Common Sense Revisited (1995)

Seek Out and Embrace The Truths
Of Reason and Common Sense.

Apply The Truths With Action.
Then You Set Yourself Free.

I dedicate this book to Thomas Paine, author of the original *Common Sense*, published as a pamphlet in 1776. Paine has been a mentor in my process of integrating the truths of America's heritage into my life, and understanding the wisdom of the Founding Fathers and the power of the *American Spirit*. When the population of the American colonies was less than five million, Paine's pamphlet sold more than 100,000 copies from January to April of 1776. Some accounts say the pamphlet had a readership of more than 500,000 (10% to 20% of the population) throughout 1776. Thomas Paine outlined several key issues later drafted into the Declaration of Independence, and *Common Sense* became a wellspring for the development of the country's individualistic *American Spirit*.

I also dedicate this to my sons, for blessing their Mom and me with their absolute trust and unconditional love. The boys are a constant reminder of the wonder, power and magic of life. They have not reached the age of having to know or address the opportunities, issues, challenges and problems that face humanity and specifically America. They are not concerned about the growing federal debt or the general erosion and apathetic separation of us from the origins of American truths, principles and values. They have the basic childhood fears. They should not be made to fear future uncertainties of our making. They naturally know they are free to pursue happiness and they can be happy with very little. As they begin to integrate into society, all the questions and lessons will begin. Within a few years, they will ask us the question that all children ask of their parents: *"Where were you when..."*

Their presence, love and trust have made us ask ourselves: *"What will be passed on to them? What is our obligation and duty?"* One's obligations to the family are first and foremost. Strong personal values springing from the love for children is the foundation that creates and supports strong communities. From strong communities come bold, courageous leaders. All of America's children deserve the best. The presence of children demands that we meet today's challenges and fulfill the honor and blessings of our American heritage and pass on to them an even better America than the great nation our forbearers passed on to us. It is for these reasons that I share these words of personal views on American truths, faith, liberty and leadership in *Common Sense Revisited*. If one saw a flash flood racing through a canyon and knew children were camping downstream, would one not find a way to warn them? The future belongs to our children. Children learn by example, by the actions of their parents and notable individuals in the community. Our actions today determine their opportunities or miseries in the future.

Children are great and wise teachers as well as willing students. They generally see all people as the same, rather than hold a prejudice because of their differences. The differences they see are the obvious and they usually ask, rather loudly, about those character traits of another person which make that individual unique. Society, on the other hand, has attempted to dampen, in the name of power, the individual spirit by martyring cultural differences instead of seeking understanding. Government has dampened individual spirit by forced, unnatural regulations.

We can learn much from children. Children do not know of *Politics A Usual*, status quo, prejudice or special interests, nor do they know how the world is complicated with egos and the ever-changing social, economic and political environments.

Examples of good citizenship for children exist in every community. Individuals with undying faith in the truths, principles and values of the *American Dream* who always remain committed and dedicated to see that America truly becomes the nation it has promised. These individuals belong to the *Faithful Majority* and they are making America's communities the way they should be. Their actions are so common, it rarely makes *prime-time news or the political polls*.

It is the *Faithful Majority*, populated by ordinary people, parents and their children, community and business leaders, who are realizing that the power in America resides with the electorate. Their votes have begun to make changes. Future votes will leave no doubts the direction in which America will proceed.

Other Acknowledgments (1995)

To Cindy for our absolute love, our two beautiful sons and for being a willing partner in creating our personal legacy. For her relentless support when needed and for knowing when the torment of authorship was real. The unknown future holds many enriching possibilities for new, exciting adventures.

There are literally hundreds of individuals who are acknowledged by the words within this book. Their influence and inspiration played like a continuous symphony while I wrote. Sometimes it was as if we were tuning up before a concert. Other times there was no way we could achieve harmony. Then there were those moments of harmonic magic that literally brought tears to my eyes. I am in awe of the relationships I share with those who are living and others who even in death continue to influence not only myself, but other current day thought Many others contributed to my life through books, magazines, newspapers, television, radio, computer and video.

No acknowledgement pertaining to a current affairs/political oriented book would be complete without acknowledging the voices of America; brought to us 24 hours a day. These are the hosts of talk radio, television and on-line computer systems, who daily open the channels of communication to the *American Spirit* in action. The multi-opinionated voices of America speak out daily regarding current events and a variety of information is delivered for review, thought and comment. The hosts provide the forum for individuals to see, hear, speak-out and discover for themselves that anyone who stands up for genuine American beliefs and values NEVER STAND ALONE.

It is Happening... (1995)

It's happening. As I near completion of this book, I am speaking with several people around the country through the Internet and as a guest of several radio talk shows. It's exciting and one can feel the energy building daily. People are making changes. They are doing what they can do, within the spirit of making things happen for the betterment of their community. The entire nation benefits. Even some political leaders are feeling it happen. Although there are only a few and their voices are calling out against a hard-driving, cold northern wind, their moment will come when the northern wind has passed, leaving one of those brisk, still evenings when a voice seems to carry forever.

What would happen if the majority of Congress threw caution to the wind, risked their political life, set aside the special interests and represented only that which would be best for all of America in the long run? As John Jay, in *The Federalist, No. II*, (1787) described the process of the Constitutional Convention in Philadelphia:

> *This Convention, composed of men who possessed the confidence of the people, and any of whom had become highly distinguished by their patriotism, virtue, and wisdom, in times which tried the minds and hearts of men, undertook the arduous task. In the mild season of peace, with minds unoccupied by other subjects, they passed many months in cool, uninterrupted, and daily consultations; and finally, without having been awed by power, or influenced by any passions except love for their Country, they*

*presented and recommended to the people the plan produced by their
joint and very unanimous councils.*

America does not need a constitutional convention, but it is in
need of *many months of cool, uninterrupted, and daily consultations;...without
having been awed by power, or influenced by any passions...* Do the
politicians have the courage, or will they hide behind the facade of
creating a new Constitutional amendment to force them to do the
job they should be doing as their duty to the American people
anyway? Where is their common sense and reason? Has it been lost
to their selfish interests as they pander to the special interests?

This Undertaking to Write this Book and its Purpose (1995)

This undertaking is to:

(1) Confirm what the *Faithful Majority* (more in the next chapter)
already know that there is a lack of reason and common sense
in American politics and government. The *Faithful Majority*
desire to make America the way it should be. They stand
awaiting the call from bold and courageous leaders moving in
the direction of realizing a new potential for the *American Spirit*
– the boldest it has ever been.

(2) Inspire the leaders to expand beyond their personal selfish and
political party special interest agendas and perform their duty
as representatives – to do what is good for all of America in
the long run. They should exhibit their courage by calling
upon the American People for assistance in resolving the
issues. The *Faithful Majority* are enriched with an abundance of
resources and infinite possibilities when called forth by a voice
of reason.

(3) Motivate those individuals who are dissatisfied with their
present situation in life, and they will stop finding someone or
something to blame. They will instead, take the actions to
improve themselves for personal benefits and for the benefit
of their family and community. They desire to achieve the
American Dream for themselves instead of feeling that they are
owed.

(4) Break through some of the tired, old barriers of frustration and anger relating to bias and prejudice. Misguided leaders, living outdated misconceptions, want many Americans to believe that they are most secure under the aid and assistance of government. The only true path to the *American Dream* is to set aside thoughts of blame and take courageous actions. Personal limitations can be overcome. Character and self esteem grow by the struggle to become the best one can be. It is never easy, but it is the American way. For anyone who begins the earnest effort of removing themselves from government dependency, they will find encouragement and moral support beyond their wildest dreams.

(5) Request all Americans to find the common ground. Even while constitutional freedoms have been declared for all Americans, many challenges remain and much work has yet to begin. The key will be the ability and the will of the Faithful Majority to deeply understand for themselves how America was founded and why. It will be necessary to know these things in order to find the common ground between so many factions. From this unknown territory of common ground, continued discussions and disagreements will develop understanding. Full understanding will take time and is only possible by working together, side by side. Further blame, by all sides of racism as cause for an individual's lack of achievement, now impedes America's progress. All Americans have equal opportunity. Government has reached its limitation to empower the individual to pursue their liberties and opportunities. Good character demonstrated by individuals within the community, personal mentoring encouragement and support will return America to its standing of greatness, *one individual at a time.* [One individual at a time is borrowed from Sue Wright, publisher of Women of Greater Atlanta. She states...*Creating excellence, one woman at time.*]

Introduction for Common Sense Revisited (1995)

There is one mind common to all individual men. Every man is an inlet to the same and to all of the same. He that is once admitted to the right of reason is made a freeman of the whole estate. What Plato has thought, he may think; what a saint has felt, he may feel; what at any time has befallen any man, he can understand. Who hath access to this universal mind is a party to all that is or can be done, for this is the only and sovereign agent.
~ Ralph Waldo Emerson ~

"Cindy, listen to this!" I would call from my home office. Cindy knew I was on my way to read her yet another passage penned by one of America's Founders, great political thinkers or philosophers. Over the course of several years[3], I have engaged in a personal study of the philosophy behind the actions of the founding and growth of America. One particular evening, I began to understand the opening quote to this Introduction. In addition, Ralph Waldo Emerson also referred to the subject of history with the following quote;

"All history becomes subjective; in other words there is properly no history, only biography. Every mind must know the whole lesson for itself - must go over the whole ground. What it does not see, what it does not live, it will not know."

History for me from elementary school through college was a realm of facts, myths and personal prejudices and opinions. Memorizing names, dates and places led to good grades. Yet, repeating from memory and good grades did not mean I knew *the whole ground* or did I fully understand the process, principles and values of America's birth, growth and development. Neither did I have real-world work experience nor had I been truly on my own to experience authentic self-sufficiency. As a student, I was fortunate to have teachers who knew that children and young adults could not fully understand nor discern the true nature,

---

3   The Author's study into the Founders began in 1990.

wisdom and actions of the Founding Fathers. My teachers did not try to teach me what I did not have the maturity or experience to understand. During the past few years[4], with personal real-world experiences, I have begun to glean some understanding of the philosophical roots of the authors of the United States Constitution, their decisions and actions as the designers of American government. While I have not been *over the whole ground*, my studies and writing have given me a much deeper sense of appreciation of America and its process of being founded, its growth and development over the past two centuries.

It was the local and national political environment and my business and community activities during election year, 1992, which motivated me further and faster into my personalized history lessons. I had built and survived a few businesses and had gained worthwhile community organization experience. I took care of daily business activities and family matters, participated within the community and turned to the various media for news. The media presented a nation in seemingly total chaos and struggle. Alarmists and extremists said America lay at the brink of disaster. Thousands of people engaged in debates, discussions, hearings, talk shows and forums[5]. Millions of dollars were spent to grandstand, politic, protest and seek advantageous positions in the topics of current affairs. The media gave the appearance that everyone and every organization was bigger than what reality would actually show. All the studies, debates, hearings, discussions, polls and conclusions still left an emptiness that was difficult to ignore. There was not any real direction and elected leaders were not leading. They were maintaining *Politics As Usual*, and otherwise appearing as if they were doing the best they could.[6]

---

4   In 2012, another seventeen years has passed – giving the Author more time to attain more understanding of the current challenges facing America and a deeper appreciation for the wisdom of American's Founders.

5   The Internet was just breaking into the general population in 1995.Prior to this; there were some computer bulletin boards and other online services accessed by modem connections.

6   Truly amazing to witness the sameness of it all over a twenty year span of time. It causes one to truly ask the questions of what drives such meaningless banter versus taking care of the business at hand. How could colonial leaders, with limited communications, develop the relationships over spans of time and distance that resulted in finding common ground for agreement on

As a parent, husband, entrepreneur and community leader, my observations of current affairs began to be shaped within the context of Ralph Waldo Emerson's quote, *"every mind must know the whole lesson for itself..."* As I would discuss with others my readings of the writings by America's Founders, it was clear that the voice of reason definitely existed in America. I also began to sense the real power and wonder of the possibilities within Joseph Campbell's quote;

> *"All people are capable of reason. That is the fundamental principle of democracy. Because everybody's mind is capable of true knowledge, you don't have to have a special authority, or a special revelation telling you that this is the way things should be."*

Taking my personal experiences, the current state of affairs in America and the Founder's political thoughts and opinions, I conjectured what America's Founders may have dealt with. What was the Founders' personal process for gaining knowledge and making choices that forwarded their personal desires for their families and communities, and what truly motivated their actions? Could it be that much different from mine?

How would the Founders relate with today's events? Most likely, they would be amazed and pleased with the results achieved from their experimental beginnings. Yet, they might be concerned to see how their predictions of factions that divide us have become reality with the institution of such powerful political machines.[7] They would be surprised to see the large numbers of government employees and appointees in non-elected positions with such sweeping degrees of power over the common individual who has been forced to pay the salaries of the unelected. They continually cautioned us regarding the wickedness of government and the tyranny that becomes possible when a faction achieves sustainable

---

complex issues of human rights, state s rights and federal authority?

7   Thomas Jefferson showed his concern of the factions that can divide us versus staying true to the common interests. *We have no interests nor passions different from those of our fellow citizens. We have the same object: the success of representative government. Nor are we acting for ourselves alone, but for the whole human race…our experiment is to show whether man can be trusted with self-government. The eyes of suffering humanity are fixed on us… and on such a theatre, for such a cause, we must suppress all smaller passions and local considerations.*

power. We have only ourselves to blame for so many bureaucrats having control over so many private individuals' lives. These non-elected officials have power that is enforced through the arrogance of an always present, yet fictitious tyrant. The non-elected officials and bureaucrats do not fear or suffer the risks of a mob (like losing their head at the guillotine).[8]

How the Founders would view current events will always be open for debate. How does the reader relate with current events in the context of the truths and principles upon which American's freedoms and liberties are based? More importantly, how many Americans have genuinely engaged them self into thinking through, on their own, versus leaving such matters to the digressions of others? The Founders came from small communities, yet they envisioned a great unified Nation that included many distinct cultures and peoples. They arrived at a consensus that worked, which took much work, time and commitment. So, it must be assumed, by Americans engaging in normal life activities of the current day that they too, can know the truths and principles as those of the Founders. There are just more people and special interests to factor into today's activities. Times have changed with many more complex relationships from our homes and across the world, but divine truths remain at the core of our souls, which are simple and await the actions of faithful people. The primary difference between then and today is that Americans are not generally putting their lives at risk on a daily basis. Natural reason and common sense exist in the majority of Americans. We have simply to make our declaration that:

"This is the way things should be!"

---

8   John Adams stated it simply relative to an individual in power without accountability. *"Power must never be trusted without a check."*

The Faithful Majority...*America's Real Power of Achievement (1995)*

The *Faithful Majority* will engage in these questions, make demands of their leaders and support those who will be genuine American leaders. The *Faithful Majority* believes in and holds dearly the truths and the myths that capture the essence of being an American, and they aspire to achieve the *American Dream*. The *Faithful Majority* resides in every American community and represents every race, gender, age, creed and culture of humanity that exists. The ranks are swelling daily as the self-employed, transitioning corporate employees, and the two-career families create better lives for themselves. The path of the *American Dream* has high hurdles and difficult struggles to leap over and break through as with the colonists who settled America and won America's independence. Government has been necessary to overcome the failings of previous laws that limited the rights to some segments of America's population. Now that their rights have been established, many individuals realize government cannot be their caretaker. These individuals are courageously accepting personal responsibility, the only true thing that will make a difference in each of their individual lives.

The *Faithful Majority* are independent, self-reliant, self-interested and willing to serve others in times of need. They work hard for what they have and expect others to do the same. They are investing personal time into professional and personal development training and they expect high returns from their efforts in the future. As more individuals realize the immense opportunities available in America, they are taking action and learning firsthand how government bureaucracies have gained too much power over an individual's pursuit of happiness.[9] The *Faithful*

---

9   Interestingly, during the past twenty years, several emerging world countries have embraced the concepts and beliefs of the entrepreneur and the American Dream. It is estimated that over one billion people will ascend to the standards of Middle Class by the year 2020 or earlier. To put this into perspective – that is double the number of Middle Class people on the planet, today (2012). It doesn't take a rocket scientist to figure out that is a whole lot of growth. Why else are major U.S. companies expanding as rapidly as they can throughout the world? When common people from around the world are asked why they have come or want to come to America, it is a

Majority are full of pride and do not seek government assistance for what they can do and should do for themselves, nor do they turn to the legal system at the drop of a hat.

The *Faithful Majority* consists of millions of individuals, who already volunteer their time, services and contribute money to support thousands of community needs and activities. They are willing to come together and sacrifice temporarily in order to replace their concerns regarding long-term safety and future security for their families. They desire the absolute best that life has to offer. These individuals do what they feel is right and accept responsibility when their actions have wronged another. Their actions over the long run will stand the test of reason and common sense. They do not protest and demonstrate disrespect for another person's property, choice of personal preferences, opinions or lifestyle. They are not the *"mob"*, which was feared by America's Founders, and their daily existence cannot possibly relate to the extremes of American lives portrayed so often on television talk shows, TV programs and movies.

The *Faithful Majority* proceed with the very reason and common sense that birthed the greatest nation on earth. They simply find a way to make things happen and do what must be done. They are ready, willing, able and excited about being a part of a new American adventure and frontier. It is their soul-filled desire which seeks to be a part of and achieve the likes of that which discovered and explored the American continent. Just as our forbearers ventured out, settled and tamed a wilderness; fought for and founded a government of the people, by the people and for the people; pioneered the America's western frontier; and put a man on the moon, the *Faithful Majority* exemplify the *American Spirit* and this spirit has been the sleeping giant. When it awakens fully and stands its tallest, our children's future will be unimaginable, just as our existence today was unimaginable by our parents. The *American Spirit* always produces heroes from the rank and file of ordinary people who have been working overtime in the past few years. The moment is near.[10]

---

single word answer – OPPORTUNITY!

10   The Author remains steadfast in his beliefs of vast array of growth possibilities for America's future. Even today, as I re-read these words

Time and again, some ordinary individual rises up from everyday living to the stature of extraordinary as originally modeled by our first President, George Washington to lead the Faithful Majority away from the factions that divide us and back to the common good. Washington exemplified the desires and dreams of America's Founders for self-government. Even in the midst of factions calling for him to become Emperor or King of America, Washington refused because he saw there were interests greater than his own or any other's self-interest; and causes nobler than personal, selfish ambition for enrichment. Washington believed and had the faith that free people could be entrusted to govern themselves and sustain the Founders' experiment of self-government. President Washington modeled his belief and faith in the American Spirit several times during his lifetime, the Revolutionary War and his presidency. Most notable when he could have taken the role of king, his actions spoke loudly as he shook the hand of the next president, John Adams and peacefully relinquished all the power and authority over the young United States.

Washington could be referred to as the Founder of the Faithful Majority. Throughout his roles in leadership, his greatness was confirmed in this thinking (through his writings) and his actions. He exemplified all the qualities we hold dear today for leaders to be – individuals with strong character, inspirational, authentic, and humble with the ability to set aside personal selfish interests for the greater good of all People.

So, where will our next George Washington rise from? The issues facing America are not issues of a particular race, gender or political party. Some will benefit more than others. It is the nature

---

written in 1995, I am in awe of the advancement in technology and vibrancy of communication through the Internet and, now, rapidly accelerating use of mobile technology. It is absolutely amazing to reflect upon these rapid advancements and how these changes only fuel the possibilities for future generations. My sons, ages 22 and 19, are full of desire and dreams to achieve even greater things than their parents. The future holds such amazing promise – and, most of all, it requires authentic leaders who will become educated to know the *whole ground*, in order to make wise decisions. It is up to the current generations, in power, to assure that our children, grandchildren and beyond are not burdened or limited by smothering Federal debts and deficits.

of society and the human condition. No re-distribution system of rich to the poor has ever existed for any length of time, no matter how it appears on paper. As with the life of Washington, there is a psyche of the hero that remains ever-present and never dies because even in the best of the re-distribution systems attempted over the past century, the result has been that those in power were the ones who benefitted. Even when Washington had many who wanted him to personally benefit by becoming King of America, he chose to remain steadfast in his faith and belief in the People. And, time and again, it is this type of hero who has emerged, eventually overcoming the systems of greed and gluttony.

Of course, the costs will be greater for some than others. Everyone has various degrees of talents, skills and knowledge. There is no place in life that nature has mandated fairness among her species, therefore, how any government can expect to legislate that which is unnatural. It is the spirit of the soul that exists within each American that will determine for him/herself where they individually will stand. It is because of this spirit and the human quality of choice that fairness and absolute equality can be neither legislated nor regulated. Notwithstanding this, an immense potential of possibilities exist, as in no other time in the history of humanity. Never before have so many of so many different races, creeds and cultures been brought together under one nation with such equality and access to opportunity as there exists today.

The *Faithful Majority* is as a sleeping giant of infinite power guarding vast resources, waiting to be mobilized into action. This giant awaits its destiny and lives for the unique experience of achieving what was once believed impossible. The possibilities are unlimited. This giant simply awaits the individuals with the faith, reverence of spirit and unselfish courage to act. The leaders who perceive what this giant can achieve and who demonstrate a true, honest, sincere, wise sense of duty, will have only to request the giant's participation. Then one day, all Americans will share the pride of those who stand within the hero's circle.

PART TWO

Essays Reflecting on Thomas Paine's Common Sense
(1995)

Author's Thoughts of Politics as Usual and its Ongoing Obsession

The Author does not think that Paine could have ever conceived the development of political parties and massive bureaucracies, nor all the lobbyists, the special interests and the media when he wrote...*Society is produced by our wants, and government by our wickedness;...* The Author also does that think Paine would be surprised by these developments and the abuses of the elected officials and their many appointees. Paine understood the design of human nature and the human condition.

Maybe Paine would have also written...*Politics As Usual is produced by our weakness of character and succumbing to the temptations of ego, wealth, the illusion of power and its influence over natural reason.* We have all known government cannot legislate and bureaucracy cannot regulate an individual's personal values, desires and dreams of becoming the best he can be.[11] Political attempts to do so have been valiant and full of compassion, yet all have been experiments and they have failed. Let us learn from the failures. The goals for equality of opportunity and compassion must remain. From dependency to opportunity is the strategy of success for all Americans. Change in politics is now necessary.

---

11 The Author wrote these words in 1995. I would have never imagined that government would attempt to legislate and regulate such simple matters of self-government like, the volume of a sugar drink an individual can buy at one time. Source – Mayor Bloomberg's sugary drink ban in New York City. When will the Faithful Majority step forward to stop such trifling, costly diatribes by political leaders swayed by some opinion poll or special interest? Where will the Faithful Majority declare such invasions to our constitutional rights must stop?

Politics is best defined as the epitome of paradox. Webster's New Unabridged Dictionary defines paradox as a statement contrary to common belief; a statement that seems contradictory, unbelievable, or absurd, but that may actually be true in fact; something inconsistent with common experience or having contradictory qualities; a person who is inconsistent or contradictory in character or behavior. Synonyms of paradox are contradiction, enigma, mystery, absurdity and ambiguity. The definition and listing of synonyms is the reality of *Politics As Usual.* John Naisbitt in *Global Paradox* writes, *At least one purpose of a paradox is to provoke fresh thinking.* There can no doubt, given the state of American affairs that fresh thinking is now absolutely necessary for America's future.

Politics As Usual is a swirling mass of people, issues and ideals. All gathered together in the tiny district of Washington, D.C. There are the temporary and the permanent individuals, the career bureaucrats, administrators and all the personnel, staff and clerical personnel within the bureaucratic organizations. The temporaries, the elected politicians (more of them should be temporary) and all their administrative assistants, staffs and clerical personnel, appointees and volunteers (praise to the few volunteers). Then you throw in the special interest organizations, lobbyists, media, attorneys, their personnel, the protestors and tourists, and you have too many people giving too much praise and pandering to present elected representatives, which creates the illusion to those in Washington they have the power. In the process, their egos have grown bigger than the electorate's checkbook.

The truth is, all these people do their jobs. Most have a sense of duty to the public, care for their families and respect others in their community. They work hard at what they do. In fact, they are also members of the *Faithful Majority.* Except they are much closer to the problems of politics and bureaucracy and yet, they do not stand up and seek to correct the problems where they see them. They, most of all, have lost their sense of personal power, choice, values that sustain the Faithful Majority and have instead grown dependent (actually enslaved) upon the system of *Politics As Usual.* This has now become a matter of survival for them.

We ordinary, common-sense folks in the real America are not really sure what anyone really does in Washington. We only hear blame and fear. The problem today is that the crowd in Washington, D.C. lives a grand illusion of power. They are constantly influencing and passing legislation. They do not have to deal with the problems and issues created by their influence or legislation. That is left up to the bureaucrats and the legal process, who likewise are not engaged in the real day-to-day activities of American community life. The communities of America are where production happens. All the while, the electorate and *Faithful Majority* continue to be force fed the illusion that things are getting done in Washington to solve the social problems, while in reality; freedoms are slowly being eaten away. The Washington people are in constant, commercially non-productive motion. Individually they are ordinary Americans, like us all. As a busy faceless mass of people, they have collectively created government into a monster of disrespect that preys upon all American people. *We, the People* have allowed ourselves to be left to suffer the miseries of this monster's mediocrity for too long.

The American electorate has figured out that too much money goes to government and too little of it gets to where it does some good. In between our checkbooks and the truly disadvantaged, which need the compassion of our hard-earned money, the money is siphoned off to feed the excessive, wasteful bureaucracies. The bureaucrats create extensive and useless forms to confuse the electorate and keep us busy and make sure we remain accountable to the government. They spend the peoples' money. They have not been held accountable to the people for how it is spent and whether or not the money produces what it was intended. All the while the *Faithful Majority* has become the servant and *Politics As Usual*, the tyrant. This tyrant has now indebted all American people over $4 TRILLION dollars.[12] A dictator could have never dreamed of creating such a form of government of tyranny or the power.

Politics As Usual is like a merry-go-round. It looks like a lot of fun, but it often makes one sick if he/she is not accustomed to always spinning rapidly and going nowhere. *Politics As Usual* has all the appearances of making something happen. More importantly, it

---

12 This $4 Trillion figure was in 1995. As a reminder, it is over $14+ Trillion in 2012. This has tripled in less than twenty years. The spiral downward has accelerated as clearly witnessed in such countries as Greece, Spain, Ireland and Italy.

keeps the merry-go-round going very fast. That way, it becomes difficult to stop, get on or get a grasp of who is really on it and what is really happening.

The status quo is the ruler of *Politics As Usual*. The status quo has the money and suggests the ways to create new legislation, refine old legislation and stall legislation, specifically campaign reform. If campaigning is reformed, this obviously threatens the financial grip the status quo maintains on politics and the politicians fear the loss of financial funding for their reelection. While their current 100 Day Dash of early 1995 has all the appearances of making things happen, it may just be whitewashing to cover up campaign and lobby reform, the culprit for maintaining *Politics As Usual*.[13]

Campaign and lobbyist regulations with their liberal loopholes allow special interests to secure huge amounts of campaign contributions to pay the huge costs of campaigning that have risen astronomically in the last decade. To pay the cost of campaigning and to get reelected, politicians spend an inordinate amount of time ingratiating anyone with the money or voter influence. It is as if, the day they are inducted into office, they immediately begin campaigning for the next election.[14] They will make appearances of separating themselves from the special interests, but they keep their hands open behind their backs.

The special interests hire lobbyists to continually remind the

---

13 Guess what? Politics As Usual continue to rule the day in 2012 and our future, unless the Faithful Majority rises up and speaks loudly and frequently. Do you want your children who are likely to burdened under massive debt to be the first generation to truly experience the downfall of America?

14 In the case of Barack Obama, he was only in office as a Senator from January 2005 to November 2008. He could not have given his full attention to the needs of his constituency because he spent much of his time as a Senator campaigning for President. In fact, he was being paid by the People for a job he did not fulfill. Instead he spent his time campaigning to achieve the Presidency. In most businesses, this type of behavior would be cause for dismissal – working or doing another job while being paid for the job hired to do, or in Obama's case, elected to do. What does that say of his or any politician's character who has found some way to justify this process? And, often these same politicians will then bring private citizens in front of a congressional hearing and chastise the private citizen for doing something similar. Where is the justice and reasoning in this?

politicians of the contributions they have received. The special interest organizations continually solicit private individuals, corporate employees and executives, who might be interested in knowing the special interest is fighting for their rights and what the concerned special interest has accomplished on *behalf of the individual.* (All the while blaming other special interests for fighting against the individual's interest. Do you think it is possible that they get together to decide who is going to fight whom, like a prizefight? No one could be that smart, or could they???) Then the special interest coaches a *minority of people* to provide grass roots activity in their communities and create numerous contacts to legislators to give it all the appearances that there is a massive groundswell of support (AND VOTES). While legislators say the money and votes do not influence them to create all these new, pork barreled, fifteen pounds of paper legislation, then I guess they really are going to reduce taxes and reduce the intrusiveness of government. Remember money, power and influence are involved, and while people have become more spiritually enlightened over the years, money and power still follow the Golden Rule of Politics. *Those who have the gold...rule.* All the while, the general Welfare of America gets put on the back burner. The reality is that they get the money and they have a power the electorate has forfeited to them. *We, the People* have become the audience of this grand illusion. They fear our participation because we will reveal their grand illusion. Yet, just as an audience can be awed by the tricks of an illusionist on stage, so it is with the Faithful Majority. How long will it be before we grow tired of such costly entertainment?

With all of this legislative activity, the elected representatives do not have the time to read or review the massive, thousands of pages of legislation. They depend upon the special interests to point out to them damaging parts that are not in the best interest of the special interest. So, the politician makes prepared speeches and creates arguments for appearance's sake and America continues to suffer. They produce their sound-bites, while believing in the ignorance or apathy of the People, who are not ignorant, but more invested in their jobs,[15] families, schools and communities

---

15   Common sense says in 2012 that politicians know the right thing to do is to focus on producing jobs as the highest priority. One would think the smart

and do not take the time to pay attention to those who are elected to represent the People.

All of this new legislation leads to growth in bureaucratic budgets. Paine wrote,

> *"...Government by kings...was the most prosperous invention the Devil ever set on foot for the promotion of idolatry. The Heathens paid divine honours to their deceased kings, and the Christian World hath improved on the plan by doing the same to their living ones."* (Thomas Paine never envisioned the tyranny of bureaucracy).

Bureaucrats gain power when politicians create new legislation. If the politicians have no time to read the legislation, they definitely do not have the time to review the regulations eventually written by the bureaucrats or their performance. What a beautiful job with the best of the best benefits, great retirement and the ability to create a job for yourself for as long as you want it. And, at no risk. Entrepreneurs and business owners can only dream of building a future of such certainty.

Maybe there should be a bureaucracy that has ultimate authority over all other bureaucracies. And, the only way this super bureaucracy can survive is that it proposes how it can bring new efficiencies and improvements to another bureaucratic organization. In effect, this super bureaucracy would perform takeovers. Some would be friendly while others would be hostile. This super bureaucracy could do as the vultures and corporate raiders did in the 1980s when they took over the bloated public companies and took action to make the companies more profitable and increase shareholders' interests. Where is this type of thinking instead of all the blaming about where and how waste exists in

---

politicians would have figured out that the more people employed, the less time they have to focus on the abuses of *Politics As Usual.* The Author asserts that is why the state of fear from Washington has cranked into action because this state of fear can draw attention away from the real issues to be addressed. Economic crisis forces *Politics As Usual* into the light of day, so politicians deflect with fear of greater losses for the People and blame others that the polls say the People are against.

government bureaucracy? The Author believes this would cause a sizeable ripple effect throughout the Federal bureaucratic system and put all bureaucrats on notice.[16]

The bureaucrat creates complex rules, regulations, codes and forms, which builds larger staffs and larger budgets. During the times of the *Organizational Man*, this type of bureaucratic structure may have been necessary. During the *Organizational Man* period, the bureaucrats displayed their power and gave the appearances of production by the numbers of people and size of budget they managed. Private corporations have proven that hierarchical structures slow the progress of innovation and burden the organizations with useless, costly and generally non-productive activity. Estimates of bureaucratic costs state that as high as seventy cents ($0.70) for every dollar ($1.00) of the budget goes for administration and salaries. That means only thirty cents ($0.30) of the people's money gets to where it is truly needed. I would adopt someone in need if all I had to pay was the thirty cents ($0.30) of the taxes I now pay.

Private Americans are generally dissatisfied with the performance of bureaucracies. Government employees are generally impersonal, slow to move and demonstrate little desire of wanting to serve the very people they are supposed to be serving. Everyone forgets who pays the salary of the bureaucrat. In fact, bureaucrats get incensed if a private citizen reminds the bureaucrat that they work for the People. When bureaucrats lose all reason, a

---

16 Why not create a Sarbanes Oxley styled regulation for government bureaucratic executives? Why not put a metric on the Benefit Recipients Satisfaction Surveys with services provided, similar to the Patient Satisfaction Surveys required of hospitals? The economic crisis has caused everyone to be forced to re-think why and how things are done and what is the result? Transparency must extend into the darkest bastions of political and bureaucratic power. The Tea Party elected representatives should become the authorities of bureaucratic systems and how to restructure those systems to fit with today's management styles and technology. These are changes that could save trillions of dollars in a short amount of time. It works for private and public companies to restructure during times of economic crisis. It is a necessity for sustainability. It will work for bureaucracies. Of course, it will result in a loss of jobs, but imagine the impact such actions would demonstrate to business owners. It would clearly communicate that government was just as interested in living within its means as private companies and individuals must do.

private individual will call upon their Congressional representative. The Congressional representative has a staff of people to deal with constituent problems. The elected politician seldom is aware of these individual constituent problems. The elected representative's staff person is delegated these problems, so the elected representative can spend their time raising more money and creating more legislation. No one ever questions the actions of the bureaucrat or the bureaucratic system nor why dissatisfaction exists.

It is time for government bureaucrats to change and if they refuse to make necessary changes and assist in removing the burdensome regulations from all Americans, then they should not be entitled to their job or position. They are servants to the people. If they do not perform their role with dignity and a sense of duty, then they should not be allowed to remain. It is time to remove the old *Organization Man* incentives and replace them with incentives for streamlining and downsizing.

Where legislation and massive bureaucratic regulations leave huge loopholes, legal questions and interpretations of distinction are necessary. Here is where the legal system (all the attorneys) gets its fair share. (Talk about a super special interest – attorneys as legislators creating broad, complex legislation that requires the involvement of the legal system. The merry-go-round is speeding up). Instead of dealing with substantive issues, courts are necessary to deal with the often-times extreme and excessive legal actions to define these new broad-brushed legislative laws and gargantuan written volumes of regulatory rules. Wide open issues are left to be resolved by attorneys representing primarily irresponsible, seemingly helpless victims that seek out the courts to resolve personal matters, instead of dealing with those matters themselves. If these victims are so helpless and disadvantaged, how have they come to be so well educated on their "LEGAL" rights and why do the attorneys receive such incredible fees? And then there is the matter when government agencies sue other government agencies. Can there be any doubt that all reason has been flung into the wind. Everyone loses, except the attorneys, at the People's expense. Remember there are a lot of attorneys in Congress.

Just when one thinks that the newest legislation will solve the problem, it actually creates more special interests groups, which adds to the complexity. One would think this design is intentional. Yet, the Author believes this *Politics As Usual* system is more like a cancer. No one really knows why it has formed. It's just there and often requires radical surgery, chemo and radiation treatments. It's time to remove the cancer of unmanaged bureaucracies. New and improved legislation is required to make changes and correct the prior injustices. And so the merry-go-round goes even faster! Just look at all the comments made by legislators over the past decade regarding new taxes and no taxes, each designed to reduce the deficit.

Obviously not all legislation is bad, but where is the wisdom and common sense today? Where is the concern for the general welfare of all American public interests? Congress is to represent the people, deliberate and act on what is good for the whole nation. They have removed the word, *"NO!!!"* from their politically correct vocabulary and allowed the extremists' rants become like the squeaky wheel. Anything to keep them quiet.

America's constitutional framework does not need fixing. The system and how the system allows politicians and the political process to be influenced is what need fixing. The temptation of special interest influence, money and vote gathering must be removed. Individual rights will not be lost, but the vices of the special interests will be restrained. Their rights, like all Americans, are guaranteed by the Constitution. The politician must return to the people of America and listen. Their public opinion polls are false by the static, cleverly crafted questions. The politicians then use the opinion polls to make their decisions, and then they use the same polls to speak to and influence the people – more merry-go-rounds.

There is tremendous wisdom and genius in America's structure of government. Gigantic problems and issues have been resolved in the past and it has been done by leaders with character, dignity and the desire to do what is best for America. Past issues and problems in America's history were resolved with fewer financial resources and fewer interested and educated people. We lack only a unified direction and a few bold authentic leaders. Currently-elected politicians have gotten lost in the social issues, which required national attention at one time, but now the special interests are simply fattening themselves and they are on a course to one day devouring even themselves for there will be no other to devour. It finally took a child to tell the Emperor he was wearing no clothes. What reason and common sense are children pointing out to you?[17]

Maybe we should listen to our children. They often know better than we the difference between right and wrong. They are taught the original Golden Rule and then they are exposed to political campaigns. What examples are we truly setting for our children? Listen to the next political campaign. Campaign advertising on television is often as irresponsible as other offensive programming. What are the children learning from these advertisements? Most likely the same disrespect as the electorate. Where will that lead America's future when several generations of Americans have been exposed to current *Politics As Usual*?[18]

The big question. Were the elections of 1994 the revolution everyone is now talking about or is this just more *political spin*? While there needs to be significantly less legislation and drastic cuts in regulations, changes require new legislation to remove much of the old. Another big question. Is old legislation being removed or

---

17   Here we are, some twenty years from the time the Author wrote these words in 1995. Things have not changed, and in fact have worsened, as it relates to *Politics As Usual*, elected officials not leading and being only selfish in their actions, bureaucracies out of control and over-regulating to gain more power and control, and the President and Congress operating such a massive government without a budget, by default – not by design deficits and debts are exploding out of control or nearing to be out of control. Bureaucracies need exceptional business managers to step in and fix the fiscal and operational issues. Lifetime bureaucrats only know they grow by adding more people and bigger budgets or they lose status and stature as a bureaucrat within the ranks of bureaucrats.

18   We now know the results on the generations after enduring all these years of such negative, blaming rhetoric of politicians and now Political Action Committees – exploding deficits and debt without any real actions being taken. In fact, the elected officials take time off to go campaign while kicking the can down the road with a hope and a prayer that things will change come November 2012. Why didn't Obama make the legislators stay in session until something was done about the coming issues of taxes for 2013? That would have required leadership, which might have made a difference for some voters. The system is broke and it needs fixing.

just mildly reformed? The status quo abhors change. What if the wolves have just adorned sheep's clothing and they hope the current electoral climate will pass soon?[19]

Wisdom and common sense have been buried by *Politics As Usual* for too long. We should not be changing the Constitution. This is another ruse by the politicians to side step their duty to the American people. Instead of displaying courage when the time for pain arrives, they cower in fear at the thought of bringing the wrath of some special interest upon themselves. There is so much that is so wrong about how this system of *Politics As Usual* operates. It is time for authentic leaders to step forward with *Politics As Unusual*. Those politicians who display wise and courageous leadership will be re-elected All the others will not.

The politicians should question their own personal desires, values, and character and if they are satisfied that their sense of duty to America is proper? Then they must seek out the common ground with all Americans. Then decide the changes to be made in all the bureaucratic structures, government programs and entitlements. The changes must result in legislative and bureaucratic changes which reduce government intrusion on the people, reduce the size of government, bring politics to the dignity it deserves and find innovative ways to preserve financial security for aging Americans and expanding opportunities for young Americans. Taxes will be significantly increased by the growth in the economy and paying off the national debt will provide for a sustainable future. *Politics As Usual* should never be the same and be replaced by *Politics As Unusual*.

Only time will tell whether or not November 1994 was a revolution that mattered. As in any business, the ultimate authority and responsibility resides with the owners. *We, the People* own this country and it is now our responsibility to see that this merry-go-round stops. Are we being attentive and responsible owners?

---

19 Sadly (there it is again) we now know the results of such empty rhetoric from 1994.

44

Background and Overview of Common Sense (1995)

While reading *Common Sense* by Thomas Paine, it occurred to me that the *voice of reason* and the general common sense appeal Paine made to the peoples of America in 1776, could speak just as clearly to Americans in the 1990's. Passages of the original *Common Sense* were relevant, even for the 1990's, while other passages needed changing and updating to relate with the current state of affairs of the 1990's in America.

Common Sense was published and distributed in early 1776. It provided a focus and direction for the colonists of revolutionary America. The colonists did not have easy lives. Life in the colonies was hard and traveling to America was done so at great risk. The stories and historical accounts of those times tell of people who were independent and self-reliant, while others were enslaved and indentured servants.* The colonists and immigrants had endured and suffered the lack of personal freedoms from their original homelands.

> *   The author is not overlooking the injustice of
> slavery and the lack of women's rights to vote.
> The laws and culture in 1776 was what it was. Just
> because those were the laws and culture of the
> time should not invalidate the achievements and
> forward movement made by leaders during these
> times. The work and sacrifices made laid the
> foundation for a variety of injustices to be
> resolved in later times. Those leaders who
> emerged stood upon the shoulders of all authentic
> leaders from the past. This Author does
> acknowledge the wisdom and the fact that
> Jefferson wrote in the Declaration of
> Independence *that all men are created equal* and the
> Constitution was approved with the language *We,
> the People...*
>
> The Author feels these were actions taken by men
> who wanted changes to made regarding slavery

and truly believed all people are created equal.
Jefferson was against slavery and was forced to
abide by the laws and culture of the times.
Thomas Paine was against slavery, cruelty towards
women and animals. While the slavery issue was
often discussed by Paine and other Founders, it
was a battle to be fought and won at a later date in
American history. It was fought and it was won. It
is time to move on.

They had survived many injustices and came to the American
colonies seeking a future and opportunity. Within the expanse of
America, the colonists had the freedom to express their
individuality. They used their natural reason and common sense,
which often times, in new and unknown surroundings meant the
difference between life and death. There was no safety net of
welfare, health insurance, unemployment wages or social security.
They made the journey to the colonies with the expectations of
pursuing their own self-interests. Self-reliance was a way of life, not
a conversation or psychology test to take. They came for known
and unknown opportunities which either did not exist from where
they came or were simply unavailable to them due to the hindrance
of social class, traditions, burdensome rules, regulations and laws.
As Paine wrote:

> *"O ye that love mankind! Ye that dare oppose, not only the
> tyranny, but the tyrant, stand forth! Every spot of the old
> world is overrun with oppression. Freedom hath been
> hunted round the globe."*

During my study of *Common Sense* and writing of *Common Sense
Revisited*, similarities of the 1770's and the 1990's became more and
more clear. Thomas Paine's *Common Sense*, impassioned by Paine's
outrage of Britain's actions at Lexington and Concord, unveiled
several myths and unreasonable traditions regarding the monarchy.
Paine's writing on the *Origin and Design of Government* also stated that
government should be *owing to the constitution of the people and not to the
constitution of the government*. Paine asked the colonists to rely on their
intuition and see for themselves the myths regarding traditions and
notice the changes that had occurred in America and throughout

the world. Paine requested that the colonists be observant of changes that were necessary for their future. The tolerant attitude of the colonists was being stretched by the laws and actions of the King of England upon the colonies. Paine questioned the reasonableness of England, a small island, ruling and protecting the American colonies, a large continent across the Atlantic Ocean. It just did not make sense.

Paine writes:

> *"As to government matters, 'tis not in the power of Britain to do this continent justice: the business of it will soon be too weighty and intricate to be managed with any tolerable degree of convenience, by a power so distant from us, and so very ignorant of us; for if they cannot conquer us, they cannot govern us. To be always running three or four thousand miles with a tale or a petition, waiting four or five months for an answer, which, when obtained, requires five or six more to explain it in, will in a few years be looked upon as folly and childishness. There was a time when it was proper, and there is a proper time for it to cease."*
> (Sounds vaguely familiar of current day bureaucracy)

Paine's reasoning and common sense became the idea and direction for the times (in 1776). The colonists began to understand and realize the reasonable course for their future lay in achieving their independence. Certain leaders within the American colonies began to see this movement among the colonists. In a letter from George Washington to Thomas Jefferson, Washington wrote, *"I find Common Sense is working a powerful change in the minds of many men."* Very soon after this observation by Washington; he, Jefferson and others began to take more deliberate action to achieve independence. The Declaration of Independence was drafted shortly thereafter, signed and delivered to the King.

In 1776, the world's economy was continuing its shift from a social system, based primarily upon land ownership by an aristocratic class to a broader group of individuals and merchants. Worldwide trade and commerce was vibrant, at the time. It is amazing to read to what extent business was transacted across the

Atlantic, in different currencies, and with communications by letters delivered by individuals after months of sailing. While American colonists who owned land had some of the appearances of the English aristocracy, it was nowhere near the same. The shifting economy was expanding by the growth of a class of merchants, traders, bankers and craftsman. The Industrial Revolution was in its infancy. Commerce was becoming an important source of wealth. While the American colonies were primarily agrarian, it was the allure of freely trading commercial goods with other nations in Europe that was one of the primary motivations of America's Founders seeking to achieve the colonies independence. Paine wrote, *"Our plan is commerce, and that, well attended to, will secure us the peace and friendship of all Europe;...*

For some colonists and immigrants, commerce became more easily attainable than ownership of land. They pursued trading with other nations, sometimes against Britain's laws. A middle class of business owners and professionals developed, as well as a working class. Government by aristocracy, feudal lords and tyranny did not suit the needs of this new developing economy, nor did the old status quo meet the wants and needs of the colonists. Unreasonable taxes and outdated laws, along with the great physical distances between England and the colonies simply were no longer efficient to meet the needs of the growing commerce and world trade in the American colonies. The physical distance and philosophical differences were now a definite hindrance to growth and development of the colonies. Although the population was primarily Anglo Saxon, the separate colonies had very distinct and separate special interests. Bringing the colonies together under some form of union (unity or cooperation) had been discussed and attempted for several years and there were a fairly equal number of Tories and Patriots. It was not until the skirmishes at Lexington and Concord and Common Sense that a single tyrant (King of England) focused the Colonists' attention that all prior actions and current actions began to say that it was only natural for the colonies to become independent. The colonists were experiencing a *confluence and convergence of choices* like no other time in the history of the world.

Similar events and shifts are taking place in the 1990's. The world's economy continues its shift from an industrial-based economy to that of an information-based, intellectual or knowledge-based economy. The industrial work force continues to shrink, as did the agrarian work force. As more of third world countries achieve the economies of the middle class, industry will grow slightly, but the real opportunities remain in the age of information. The professional and business owner class is growing rapidly, as it did in the 1770's. More and more individuals own their own business or have part-time businesses. Small businesses are conducting business locally and globally. The formation of businesses in the arena of information and knowledge are exploding, uncovering new opportunities and spawning a vast array of new resources to pursue many other vast opportunities. Just as the King and government of England could not control or have full knowledge of what was transpiring in the colonies, neither can a modern-day government seek to control or know everything that is transpiring in the information era. Economic and social changes are once again creating new opportunities and there is the need for change in government.

New technologies are increasing productivity of individuals, bringing major corporate employment downsizings. This is again causing major shifts in the general population. Just as immigrants and farmers learned to work in the factories, industrial based employees today are learning new, productive knowledge and skills. Telecommunications are moving even greater portions of the employment base from the cities into the suburban areas and even out into rural areas. As the colonies had distinct and diverse interest, so are there distinct cultures in every American community. As in 1776, it is time for these diverse, separate interests to come together for the benefit of the whole nation.[20]

---

20   Just as the Author could see the similarity of the times as Paine wrote in Common Sense in 1776, it is interesting for the Author to re-read what he wrote in 1995 and now know, by covering the whole ground, during this past twenty years and see the results of the times in the 1990s to the times in 2012. It makes me wonder what Thomas Paine felt by knowing that his Common Sense had such an impact upon the way of life for so many within a few years after Common Sense was published. I believe that we are living in the midst of great change, once again. I believe it is the vibrancy of the communications, availability of information and transfer of knowledge through the Internet, today (2012).

A capitalist, representative democracy will stand through these times of change, but the infrastructure of a government stagnated by centralization and laden with the enormous size of bureaucratic agencies simply does not suit the needs or the wants of the people. The complexity, control and lack of implementing and leveraging new technologies creates a needless dependency by people who live in the midst of this chaos of change and complexity and, by the birthrights they share because of the U.S. Constitution and Bill of Rights, Americans naturally cherish independence most of all.

What is Common Sense? (1995)

Over the last few years, the words *common sense* has often been used in political rhetoric. The word *common* is defined by Webster's New Universal Unabridged Dictionary, as being of or relating to a community at large; public; widespread; general – such as common knowledge. The word *sense*, is defined as a meaning conveyed or intended...consciousness, sanity, consensus, sentience, intelligence...sound mental capacity and understanding. Therefore *common sense* suggests that any individual, who exercises the ability to observe the general nature of current surroundings and circumstances (those items that are commonly seen by many) and then applies reasonable mental capacity, has the ability to understand what is happening and what it means for their personal lives, their families, businesses, job and community. Everyone has common sense available to them, if they choose to use it. We know that when the colonists matched their common sense (observing and communicating with passionate discourse with others in similar situations) with their knowledge, experience, wisdom, passion and personal desires, history now reveals that the greatest nation ever conceived achieved a status unmatched by any other nation.

No one can doubt the knowledge and experience that exists in the American people today. It is time to utilize our common sense to determine the best and wisest application of the extensive knowledge and experience available to so many, today. If the politicians are going to use it in their speeches, then they should apply it in their actions.

A Great Political Essay (1995)

Common Sense is one of America's great political essays. Truths never change. While life's situations and circumstances are constantly changing, the truths which Thomas Paine put forth in 1776 stand clear and present, even given America's situation today. The phrase common sense is often used in sound-bites from political leaders. What was the role of common sense in the founding and subsequent growth and development of the United States? Common sense truths and wisdom are ever-present in the majority of Americans and when the occasion arises for action; swift, determined action is taken, so that the principles and values of liberty and freedom are sustained in the present and for all future generations. It is our duty to do our part in maintaining the true destiny of America. It lies deep within our heritage of hope and faith in us and God.

The writing *Common Sense* by Thomas Paine once empowered the peoples of America to take courageous actions to fight and win individuals' rights for liberty and freedom. During a time of uncertainty and crisis, Paine's *Common Sense* called for a declaration of independence that would guarantee freedom, property and the right to worship according to one's conscience. His writing captured the early developing *American Spirit* of individualism, optimism and pride for independence. It is time once again for common sense to empower the *American Spirit*.

Future changes should not seek to damage or remove accomplishments achieved in the arena of human rights, while laws and regulations that no longer make sense must be changed. The sweeping changes to be expected to change are the methods and systems being utilized to now further all American's rights of equal opportunity. Certain political methods, entitlements and bureaucracies have served their purpose. It is now time for society to reclaim its role and to forward the process of defining and drawing distinctions to understand and establish who we are as individuals and as a nation, in these new and rapidly changing times of the 1990s. America remains the world's leader. The framework of American democracy is sound and proven. It is our privilege to use it to its fullest extent and our duty to make it the best it can be. It is vital for us to first stand true to our heritage, rights and

51

freedoms to arrive at solutions from the common sense, heart and soul of the American Spirit before attempting to strip away the very foundation that has supported all that has been built.

It is in Thomas Paine's *Common Sense* and the writings of several other Founders that the Author first came to realize the birth of America came from the thoughts, education, knowledge and ideas of the Founders with a strong dose of passion, courage, leadership, self-reliance and individualism. The design and structure of American government was the result of the Founders thinking through all the challenges, hopes and dreams. Common sense became more of an ability or skill to develop than two words to describe one's state of mind. Thomas Paine captured the heart, mind, soul and common sense of the colonists in his published works of *Common Sense*.

The following chapter contains direct passages from Thomas Paine's original *Common Sense*, published in 1776. Additional writings, notations and comments are made by the Author as of 1995. The value to the reader is to embrace the thoughts of Thomas Paine to glean deeper understanding for what truly drove the times and events of 1776 and beyond. Use the Author's notes and comments for exercising your own personal thoughts, not to believe as the Author, but to develop your own thoughts, beliefs and values based upon whom you are. You (the reader) are unique with very different experiences, knowledge, skills and talents than the Author. The value of this reading process is to encourage you to experience, for yourself, the truths that drive the America Spirit.

The following chapter, *On the Origin and Design of Government in General* is not the complete text of this segment of *Common Sense*. These passages have been selected for the purpose of giving the reader some basis in Paine's very basic philosophies of simple government. The Author believes these are important for the Faithful Majority to be informed and *cover the whole ground* to have full understanding and appreciation of their American heritage and for thinking and acting during the challenging times Americans and political leaders face today.

How Simple Can It Be (1995)

Millions of people have already been in action for years and thousands are joining these ranks daily. Without ceasing religious and community organizations with deep history of compassion, community improvement and support of personal development, shine brightly. These organizations are expanding in scope; remain focused on serving humanity and are devoid of political agendas. Personal sense of self-worth will be sustained by the personal efforts of each unique and distinct individual, which will make a difference for another individual.

The political organizations, designed and maintained, and that say they will deliver the message for you simply are a part of the system that is not working. They seek your money and your vote, which buys them personal, self-interested power in Washington, at the People's expense. Many have ambitions for ever-increasing roles of power and authority. How can such ambitious self-interests be mindful of the needs of the many that have elected them into their role?

A New Order of Authentic Thought Changed the World (1995)

The Founders saw the need for a new order of government. Although untested, it seemed just and right. Their wisdom and actions, and the actions of all succeeding generations have become the reality that exists for all Americans today. It was impossible in 1776 to imagine what America would become. The founding structure for the government of America was an experiment, but an experiment in which the Founders truly believed. Their beliefs were based upon the current events of the time, their education, personal experiences and personal thoughts regarding their values and ideals. Their thoughts and ideals may have been political theories then, but the American experiment now stands when all other political theories have long fallen.

Colonists took uncommon actions to build, often from nothing, to have the lives they desired. The individuals within the colonies of America then arrived at a point of decision. They could choose to declare independence or not. They chose independence. The ramifications of not doing so we will never know, but I assert the results achieved in the world by Americans would not have evolved and the potential and opportunities that lay before Americans today would not exist. Past history will not solve the issues America faces today, and neither can the status quo do what is right for America's future. The challenge that stands before every American is the willingness to reclaim America's heritage and the *American Spirit* for themselves.

This book seeks to inspire all Americans to set aside their personal judgments of historical events and draw forth from themselves that which is uncommon and with a calling to their duty to make things the way they should be. We do not have to storm Washington. We simply have to continue leading by our actions in our own communities, take personal responsibility for our lives and exercise our power of the freedom to express our voice with our vote. Many have died for us to have this freedom to vote.

We have the benefit of reading and grasping the Founders' thoughts and ideals. We can correlate those with the times in which we are living. We have the freedom to read, study, discuss and integrate the better parts of their wisdom and teachings. The personal mistakes and human rights injustices by the Founders are not to be ignored, yet neither do we have the right to pass judgment. We were not there. We did not live the lives they chose, nor the laws placed upon them. Whatever their chosen lifestyles and beliefs, do not diminish the truths for which they risked their lives. The freedom to study and understand the origin of America's freedoms is truly a blessing. Our lives are enriched and we are inspired to become the best we can be.

The better each American, the stronger the families.

The stronger the families, the stronger the communities.

The stronger the communities, the bolder our leaders.

The Matter At Hand (1995)

The matter at hand is unity and collaborative participation. As in nature, where the great Mississippi River and the Ohio River converge, there is a distinct line of demarcation. Where the waters of the two great rivers converge, there is tremendous turbulence, yet the waters from each river do not mix together. Rather, it is further downstream before the separate rivers' waters actually mix together and become one. America seems to be at a similar point of convergence and confluence. The old status quo and the emerging status quo are converging and there are distinct lines of demarcation, creating tremendous turbulence and chaos in almost every aspect of society and government. The old seeks to maintain their position of power – the emerging seeks to gain the position of power.[21] There can only be one natural outcome. As with the great rivers, the two will become one. Both will become the new status quo. They must simply flow along the side of the other for a distance, in order to begin to understand the purpose and motivations of each other.

The differences regarding the methods of achieving what is best for America have made for heated debates. Given the intensity of the debates over the past thirty years[22], America should expect only the best outcomes to be realized. But, continued debates now will only delay America's progress. My personal thoughts and philosophical views on America's current state of affairs seek not to fuel the fires of blame[23], but rather to assist the reader in

---

21   It can now be seen as those emerging into power, there will be mistakes and new ideologies tried, but something exists within America that cannot be denied, both from a divine perspective and the desires and dreams of those who remain faithful to the possibilities and opportunities this great nation has for all who genuinely believe in the American rights to *Life, liberty and the pursuit of happiness…*

22   This time is now almost fifty years that the divisions of factions have held America hostage to its once highly regarded status of greatness – admired and revered by others around the world who seek to be here in America for one reason. Opportunity exists here like nowhere else in the world.

23   It is a sad note to see those who have been elected to get the job done; and how much time they actually waste blaming and finger pointing just to grab a personal sound-bite to be replayed many times over until you hear others

acknowledging the truth and do what they feel is right for America. While specific blame is easily found in selected, out of context situations, the truth is that we are all to blame for the situations America faces today – from the outright scandals in all levels of government to the electorate not voting or casting under-educated votes. I seek to find that fertile ground within the reader's mind, heart and soul, in the hope that the seeds of the truths and principles in these writings will sprout and nourish the reader's duty as an American to become a part of the resurgence of the *American Spirit* that has made this the greatest country on earth. If not so, why do so many from other countries desire to be here? The direction for America is absolutely pre-determined by the United States Constitution. *We, the People* must regain our power and choose unity and collaborative participation.

America will survive the present challenges and chaos. The outstanding quality of being human is the power of choice. Humanity will move forward. America has moved forward rapidly several times in the past, when faced with the crisis of war and depression. Neither of these stands at America's threshold today. Tremendous opportunities stand at America's threshold and the choice of a future lies within those leaders from American society and government, who will step forward with the convictions and commitment of the Founding Fathers. The peoples of America are calling for current day leaders in every community throughout America to observe the truths, think with reason and common sense and take the necessary actions that are needed for today.

The real power that exists in America today will reveal itself in America's future history. Yet, it is the daily actions of each and every American that will bring forth desired outcomes. The electorate power has spoken in the recent elections of 1992 and 1994.[24] The elected politicians say they have listened. The tasks are

---

begin to express such statements. Sadly those who espouse these sound-bites do so with little personal *thinking through* for themselves. They are simply parroting what they have heard like a young child speaking out what they hear from their parents.

24   Similar to the mid-term elections of 2010 – the rising up of the Tea Party considered by many as a clear voice against the current administration's direction and for this Author, some hope that the Faithful Majority is close

many, and *We, the People,* who have the ultimate authority and responsibility must remain ever-vigilant during these times of change. Old habits are not easily broken.

Getting the Job Done (1995)

In the congressional elections of 1994, the American electorate expressed its desire for elected leaders to step forward boldly and get the job done. Commitments, contracts and promises were made during the campaign. The newly elected Congress seems to be making the attempts, and yet *Politics As Usual* maintains a tight grip by not allowing natural reason and common sense to become a guiding light upon the issues that face America.[25] At the same time Americans must develop more fully their responsibilities in the matters at hand. If the actions of the electorate wane from the majority of Americans and Americans do not step forward responsibly, *Politics As Usual* will do as it has always done.

It is my hope that *Common Sense Revisited* will be a voice of reason to all Americans and specifically to the elected leaders, so they may truly take to heart the message of the elections of 1994 and become those leaders that seemingly come from nowhere, when America is in the time of need. If not, then in future elections, there can be no doubt of where the majority of Americans stand. This is the blessing of the American way.

---

behind to fulfilling its responsibilities. Such is the brilliance of the Founders' design. The challenge for the Tea Party – can they overcome the status quo? Do they have the ability to engage the *Politics As Usual* and be the leaders called to fulfill the duty of elected officials or will the status quo win once again – at America's loss. The Tea Party's only hope is that it becomes clear to the status quo of *Politics as Usual* that the Faithful Majority have truly embraced the ideals of self-government and the Tea Party is not just another faction or special interest, soon to fade away. The Tea Party or some other party must be the one to lead other factions toward the common ground and common sense.

25   The issues are not much different and the size of the issues have exploded in scope and costs. *Kicking the can down the road* has become a common statement, during current times (2012). Will the leadership emerge or not, is the real question.

My desire is that the reader will seek the truths and access the universal mind Ralph Waldo Emerson makes reference to in the opening quote of this Introduction. Also, the reader should exercise their God-given ability to reason and read within the context of Paine's request of his readers in 1776,

> *"that he* (the reader) *will divest himself of prejudice and prepossession, and suffer his reason and his feelings to determine for themselves; that he will put on, or rather that he will not put off, the true character of a man, and generously enlarge his views beyond the present day."*

While answers to America's current issues are not spelled out in the Founders' writings, the reader will discover common ground, *the whole ground,* in which to relate the Founders situations with today's. The truths, principles and values upon which America has been founded are revealed and the reader will access the same wisdom of reason and common sense that birthed the greatest nation on earth. The reader will shift from being one to say, *"Things are not right"* to saying *"This is the way things should be."* Those who are committed will gain this wisdom. They will also gain the power to achieve for themselves, their family, their community, state and nation. Herein lays the true meaning of the birthright gifted to all humanity by America's Founders.

The Questions Remain (1995)

What are the role of government and the role of society? What are the real issues? Who is telling the truth? What has been done before? Is it government's role to make life more equal, more fair and by whose standards; or should government provide a generally secure environment for all committed Americans to pursue the opportunities that lay before them?

These questions are but a few and none have easy answers. Allowing these questions to remain requires different thinking so that the diverse American cultures might begin pulling together to create unified solutions. The continuation of the dissension and arguments along political party lines, special interests and cultural distinctions would be like forcing the waters of the Mississippi and

Ohio to remain separate all the way to the Gulf of Mexico. That would be unnatural and nothing would be achieved by remaining separate during times following great turbulence and chaos.

Open-ended questions lead everyone into the realm of reason and common sense. From there the truths emerge, declarations are made, commitments are given, people are inspired and the necessary actions are taken. Some of the actions will succeed and some will fail. Those who make the commitment stand together. Some grow weak – others grow stronger. Some fade away – others, with new resources appear. Some go the other way – those remaining may have to retreat and renew for brief periods and then re-emerge with new strengths and resources to get the job done.

From the Appearances of Apathy to the Power of Alliance (1995)

As understanding begins replacing myths and mis-understandings and it becomes more clear who and what Americans have become over the last thirty years, what appeared as apathy in the electorate will surge forth as a new, loosely organized, free-flowing, powerful alliance.[26] America's leaders will regain their courage, breaking free from the special interests, and return to their duty as representatives to all American interests for the long run. Common sense and the voice of reason will replace the smothering bureaucracies and regulations that have made Americans part-time indentured servants to the tyranny of *Politics As Usual*.

As the tide rises, a tidal wave builds deep in the ocean of all Americans' souls.[27]

---

26 The Author reminds the reader to reflect upon how the current day Tea Party evolved. From loosely organized gatherings, powerful alliances have emerged to drive forth an agenda to reveal and release the *American Spirit*. Is it sustainable or will it just become another faddish faction of politics?

27 Today (2012) these tidal waves from deep in the ocean have been more thoroughly researched as tsunamis, capable of incredible power and strength, witnessed by the vast destruction to Japan. Clearly, a tsunami represents a power of such magnitude that any attempt by man to stop it is futile. Such is the way of the *human spirit*, gifted to us by God and proven time again

The strengths of America's cultural diversity will be fully understood and new resources will be discovered to resolve society's major social issues that have tarnished the *American Dream*. Individuals, even those labeled as disadvantaged, are achieving the *American Dream*, where it was once before considered *The Impossible Dream*. The lighthouse beacon of America's destiny has never, never faded, no matter the desires and designs of an ambitious few, who find their way into positions of authority and power. This beacon has shown the way for all prior generations of Americans and it now shines brightly from the heartland of America. Where politics and bureaucracy have often failed, the *American Spirit* has always, always, always achieved success.

So What Can You Do? (1995)

The Political Courage Index

Support those national, state and local politicians who exhibit the courage and do their duty as expected in their position of being an elected representative of the people. This is not an issue of right versus left, nor right versus wrong. There is no doubt the tidal wave approaches. The leaders to be remembered are those who ride the wave, point in the direction it is going and truly live the principles and values the *Faithful Majority* live and breathe every day of their lives.

If the current government programs, philosophies and actions were still working, we would not be having these discussions and there would be no approaching tidal wave of change. Such is the nature of humanity.

How does one recognize political courage? Consider the politician who continues to blame and ridicule (whether from the right or left) to prove a point; this is not courage.[28] Instead,

---

throughout all of recorded history.

28 The Author must call attention to the blatant and continued use of blaming others during the current election process of 2012. The Faithful Majority believe in a leader who, like themselves, will take personal responsibility for the situation they have stepped into. Elected leaders clearly chose to pursue the role of a politician. Any such elected official who continues to blame

recognize those politicians who take a stand and then begin walking in a direction that encourages others, representative of the majority, to fall into step. Together they will move the nation.[29]

Only For an Individual to Do (1995)

The time to wait was yesterday.[30] Today, one individual, whether a spoken word by a known leader or a neighbor extending their hand in full humanly compassion to one in need, could in reality create the defining moment for any number of positive outcomes. Hopes only power rests in our collaborative actions

---

others for whatever the situation has clearly not taken responsibility for the role they have. This inability to be responsible and call forth the greatness of America clearly demonstrates they are not an authentic leader who stands in the midst of the issues and makes the decisions, that while may not, fit the polls, but in the end, prove the right course of action. Such leaders as Lincoln and Truman. Imagine the situations they stepped into! And our leaders today cannot step up to these times? Who will be the leader to emerge and be admired for decades and centuries to come, as we admire the leadership, character and maturity of George Washington.

29 Throughout American history, Americans have experimented with making vast changes in political thought. Such changes have often made great strides in changing prior, unacceptable prejudices and bias of injustice to humanity. The Author believes the election of 2008 was such an experiment. While an amazing statement and giant leap for mankind to elect a black president of the United States, it cannot be considered a racial prejudice to proclaim the qualifications and quality of leadership are not to be confused with excellent oratory skills. An authentic leader does not allow being blown around like a rudderless sailboat. Nor, continue to find blame with whatever group that appears as an easy target to make certain voters believe their individual problems are caused by "The Man." Blaming others is the sign of extreme weakness. These are not times for weak leadership. These times demand leaders with the courage who will stand up and declare responsibility for the situation at hand and call forth the best of all Americans to move forward in unity and cooperation.

30 Sadly, this was written in 1995. Seventeen years, America has waited. Yes, vast progress has been made for many. But, the core of the issue, entitlements has not been addressed in a way that secures the financial future of America and provides an appropriate structure for American enterprise and entrepreneurs to be fully supported to compete on the world stage.

today. Tomorrow remains the possibility and our faith fuels the eternal flame of liberty.

And Battle Lines Will Be Drawn (1995)

There are many complex issues to be addressed. Many cannot see, nor do they want to see things being the way they should be, especially if it does not fit their picture of the way they want things to be. There will be the discussions and demonstrations of losers and winners. These discussions and demonstrations simply maintain the present state of affairs in America. For these reasons, the Author requests the reader to take action on the following:

Be a registered voter. Call or write a simple statement to the politicians of your community, state and national governments. Let them know you are watching and listening. Let them know your vote will be cast for the results of their actions and no amount of political rhetoric or millions of dollars of advertising will ever loom greater than determined actions grounded in natural reason and common sense.

Some of the results *We, the People* desire for the nation will take time to develop. Natural reason and common sense are the birthright of humanity and our Founding Fathers created a system of government which allows the people and their freedom to express this birthright to the fullest. We already know the distinctions. We simply have to cast an educated vote. Authentic American leaders will decide for that which is only natural for America.

PART THREE

Thomas Paine's Common Sense Adapted
for 1995

On the Origin and Design of Government in General

> *Common Sense* by Thomas Paine, as originally
> published in 1776 with some adaptations and
> updating of language. Author's Notes by Alan W.
> Goldsberry

Some writers have so confounded society with government, as to
leave little or no distinction between them; whereas they are not
only different, but have different origins. Society is produced by
our wants, and government by our wickedness; the former
promotes our happiness positively by uniting our affections, the
latter negatively by restraining our vices. The one encourages
intercourse, the other creates distinctions. The first is a patron, the
last a punisher.

> Author's Note: There are special interests today
> which believe that government should create the
> *Great Society*. Where is Paine's wisdom today?
> While the resources of government, through taxes,
> can provide broad social needs to the
> disadvantaged, society itself is the first choice of
> *patron*. As it has now been realized, most of the
> social programs of government are in chaos,
> costly, wasteful and ineffective. The programs
> have even become punishers of the disadvantaged,
> in reality enslaving them instead of truly serving
> them in ways that meet their needs. This is

society's role. While it may appear government can create the *Great Society*; in reality history now reveals the grand designs of the *Great Society* now punish and enslave not just those receiving the benefits, but now punish and enslave even those who pay their taxes to provide for the needs of others. It is time for the patrons to unite. The Author refers to the patrons as the Faithful Majority.

Society in every state is a blessing, but Government, even in its best state, is but a necessary evil; in its worse state an intolerable one: for when we suffer, or are exposed to the same miseries by a Government, which we might expect in a country without a Government, our calamity is heightened by reflecting that we furnish the means by which we suffer. Government, like dress, is the badge of lost innocence; the palaces of kings are built upon the ruins of the bowers of paradise. For were the impulses of conscience clear, uniform and irresistibly obeyed, man would need no other lawgiver; but that not being the case, he finds it necessary to surrender up a part of his property to furnish means for the protection of the rest; and this he is induced to do by the same prudence which in every other case advises him, out of two evils to choose the least. Wherefore, security being the true design and end of government, it unanswerably follows that whatever form thereof appears most likely to ensure it to us, with the least expense and greatest benefit, is preferable to all others.

Author's Note: Taxes are necessary for providing for the nation's security. Yet, it is not possible for government to be all things to all people. It must seek to provide for the greatest benefit, allow the individual to choose for himself and trust in society to address individual needs and wants of those temporarily disadvantaged members of society. The current design of American government, which is to have elected representation, has attempted to be the caretaker. It is time for all Americans to accept their personal responsibility in the matters of society. It is time for us to also be prudent in our matters of government. The electorate's responsibility is to remain vigilant over the representatives. The electorate has failed in its responsibility. It is time for change and the change is the awakening of the Faithful Majority – those who understand the heart, soul, mind and common sense of the American Spirit.

...If the colony continue increasing; it will become necessary to augment the number of representatives, and that the interest of every part of the colony may be attended to, it will be found best to divide the whole into convenient parts, each part sending its proper number: and that the elected might never form to themselves an interest separate from the electors, prudence will point out the propriety of having elections often: because as the elected might by that means return and mix again with the general body of the electors in a few months, their fidelity to the public will be secured by the prudent reflection of not making a rod for themselves. And as this frequent interchange will establish a common interest with every part of the community, they will mutually and naturally support each other, and on this, depends the strength of government, and the happiness of the governed.

Author's Note: Paine wrote of the concepts of representatives and the necessity of the representatives mixing with the general body of the electorate. But, as we now are aware, Congressional members have created fiefdoms for themselves. They have become career politicians with large congressional staffs to interchange with the common interests of the community. Where Paine says, *"...not making a rod for themselves."* The Author notes that rod, according to Webster's New Universal Unabridged Dictionary means a kind of scepter or badge of office; hence, royal power or authority. The wisdom of America's Founders is truly amazing. America's leaders had it once. America will have it again. The electorate, the Faithful Majority, must make this happen.[31]

Here then is the origin and rise of government; namely, a mode rendered necessary by the inability of moral virtue to govern the world; here too is the design and end of government, viz. Freedom and security. And however our eyes may be dazzled with show, or our ears deceived by sound; however prejudice may warp our wills, or darken our understanding, the simple voice of nature and reason will say, 'tis right.

I draw my idea of the form of government from a principle in nature which no art can overturn, viz. that the more simple any thing is, the less liable it is to be disordered, and the easier repaired when disordered;

> Author's Note: Proponents for remaining with the political state status quo say that due to the complexities of government, career politicians are necessary. It is time for those politicians who continue to believe this way, to be removed in order for the complexities to be removed. It is time for simplicity to rule, not elected officials who complicate for their selfish benefit.

---

31   The Author can only continue to emphasize this reality of how the elected have become their own distinct culture and social status. While they argue and blame over healthcare and retirement programs for Americans, they have created the best of the best health care and retirement benefits for themselves. Just as Paine said they would. How can this be that elected officials with a duty to serve have, in reality, created themselves as a privileged class, while they hold Americans hostage with their ongoing and incessant indecisions and significant lack of authentic leadership. It is by the elected officials design to use the power given to them to serve their selfish interests. How long will the Faithful Majority stand for such abuse of power and how they mock the very gifts given to Americans by the sacrifices of so many.

Some Additional Thoughts of *Politics as Usual* and its Ongoing Obsession (1995)

> This is another revision, adaptation and update by the Author from the original Common Sense, On the Origin and Design of Government in General...

We, the People have been willing participants in *Politics As Usual*. Our hearts and souls have been thinly veiled with hopeful, unrealistic expectations of politicians' promises that government would care for society's ills. Society is produced by our choices and desires, and government by our consumption. During the last thirty years, in the midst of incredible worldwide social, economical, environmental and political changes, our freedom has still resulted in wonderful achievements of wants and desires beyond anyone's expectations. At the same time, social issues and problems exist in embarrassing abundance. We willingly transferred and filtered our compassions through government's great society programs and its bureaucracies. This has left us personally unacquainted and struggling to understand the cause and solutions for America's social issues and problems. We have so confounded society with government, as to leave little or no distinction between them. We have been willingly seduced, wishing for a patron, but we now see that government has become our enslaver.

The choices of our *pursuits of happiness* available within a free society is a blessing, but government, even in its best state, is but a necessary evil. Now, *Politics As Usual* has become a tyrant, utilizing government as its instrument of power to intrude into every aspect of American life, bringing upon the people excessive taxes, bureaucracies, regulations and an unconscionable federal debt. As we reacquaint ourselves with our responsibilities as the electorate for a government of the people, by the people and for the people, our concerns are magnified by reflecting that we have furnished the means by which these issues and problems exist. While the social, economic, environmental and political issues of society and government reach every corner of the world, extremists of opposite ends of the political spectrum cry out for no government or absolute government. Neither of these is valid and has little chance of occurring as long as the *Faithful Majority* remains vigilant. The people are willing, within reason, to surrender a part of their earnings to accomplish that which is stated in the Constitution of the United States; *to form a more perfect Union, establish Justice, insure domestic Tranquility, provide for the common defense, promote the general welfare and secure the blessings of liberty to ourselves and our posterity.* We are motivated to do this to maintain personal choices and self-interests of life, liberty and the pursuit of happiness. The true design of American government is stated in the Constitution, without question, *Politics As Usual* must refuse its old ways and establish the government systems that most likely will insure these promises to the people with the least expense and greatest benefits. Government should act in moderation; Society must remain vigilant and responsible.

In a free society, government cannot be all things to all people. The Founders feared that elected representatives and special interests, with no ill intentions in the beginning, would become familiar with one another by the very nature of their contact and potentially would work together for their own personal gains, as opposed to the good of the nation. As Jefferson remarked,...

> *Mankind will soon learn to make interested uses of every right and power which they possess, or may assume. The public money and public liberty...will soon be discovered to be sources of wealth and dominion to those who hold them; distinguished, too, by this tempting circumstance, that they are the instrument, as well as the object, of acquisition. With money we will get men, said Caesar, and with men we will get money. Nor should our assembly by deluded by the integrity of their own purposes, and conclude that these unlimited powers will never be abused, because themselves are not disposed to abuse them. They should look forward to a time, and that not a distant one, when a corruption in this, as in the country from which we derive our origin, will have seized the heads of government, and be spread by them through the body of the people; when they will purchase the voices of the people, and make them pay the price.*[32]

---

32   Who is willing to deny the abilities of the Founders to think through the

Here then, along with society's apathy to its duties as the electorate, *Politics As Usual*, being left to its own devices too long, has created a behemoth of government in which the Founders would say, *"We told you so."* We can look back and see that while it may have begun with all good intentions, it now exists with little, if any, common sense. The temptations of the Peoples' money, most likely, would test anyone of any gender, race, creed or culture. However, *Politics As Usual* will continue to dazzle our eyes with its flag-waving and our ears will be subjected to undignified and blatant misuse of *spins and sound-bites* to avoid the real campaign issues. We must demand they get the job done regarding their promises of lowering taxes, reducing the size of government and regulations, relinquishing all the congressional special privileges and removing the influence of special interests, bureaucrats and unelected representatives. Whatever one's political party affiliation, know and absolutely understand some factions of the party will work hard to prejudice your understanding that the status quo must survive. Yet, the simple voice of nature and reason that has been a whisper in the dark will become louder and more clear as the *Faithful Majority* stand and say, *"This is the way it should be."*

Of Monarchy and Hereditary Succession (1995)

> Author's Note: America does not have a monarchy or hereditary succession, yet there exists some elements of these in American politics. I have included these passages for information to assist one's observation of the American

---

eventual consequences of individuals in government and the outcomes for the People? Based upon this writing by Jefferson, it is clear of his education and knowledge and his command of common sense. At the same time, his writing demonstrates his ability to think through the eventuality of corruption in any government. It is the Author's ambition that more people realize these simple truths written by Jefferson, Paine, Washington and other Founders in order for the Faithful Majority to develop similar abilities as Jefferson to bring common sense to these chaotic times of uncertainty and fear.

equivalent of a Monarchy, referred to as *Politics As Usual*. Thomas Paine saw opportunity for America by realizing that the monarchy and hereditary succession were not a matter of birthright and it made no sense for. He wrote that the Monarchy was an:

..."insult and imposition on posterity. For all men being originally equals, no one by birth could have a right to set up his own family in perpetual preference to all others forever, and tho' himself might deserve some decent degree of honors of his contemporaries, yet his descendants might be far too unworthy to inherit them.

Author's Note: Paine's original thoughts regarding the monarchy and hereditary succession is best shown in the following passages. When this writing is put into the perspective of why term limits are reasonable and beckon to our common sense, one truly begins to see the power of Paine's writings and why it sold 500,000 copies during a time in which it took mail weeks and months to reach its destination.

This is supposing the present race of kings in the world to have had an honorable origin: whereas it is more than probable, that, could we take off the dark covering of antiquity and trace them to their first rise, we should find the first of them nothing better than the principal ruffian of some restless gang, whose savage manners or pre-eminence in subtlety obtained him the title of chief among plunderers: and who by increasing in power and extending his depredations, overawed the quiet and defenseless to purchase their safety by frequent contributions... Perhaps the disorders which threatened, or seemed to threaten, on the decease of a leader and the choice of a new one (for elections among ruffians could not be very orderly) induced many at first to favor hereditary pretensions; by which means it happened, as it hath happened since, that what at first was submitted to as a convenience was afterwards claimed as a right.

Authors Note: While America is not under the rule of a monarchy, there have been instances in American politics that a particular family has second and third generation politicians. While those individuals must still be elected, the electorate should be more vigilant and not elect on namesake, but be cautious of the candidate's mastery of *Politics As Usual*. Blind acceptance to favor hereditary pretensions has led to the ruin of nations.[33]

But it is not so much the absurdity as the evil of hereditary succession which concerns mankind. Did it ensure a race of good and wise men it would have the seal of divine authority, but as it opens a door to the foolish, the wicked, and the improper, it hath in it the nature of oppression. Men who look upon themselves born to reign, and others to obey, soon grow insolent. Selected from the rest of mankind, their minds are early poisoned by importance; and the world they act in differs so materially from the world at large, that they have but little opportunity of knowing its true interests, and when they succeed to the government are frequently the most ignorant and unfit of any throughout the dominions.

Authors Note: How many of our elected politicians today are *poisoned by importance?* We know by listening to them in how they speak so differently and act differently than the world at

---

33   Current elected officials in 2012, step into a system of hereditary design. Elected politicians have created this abusive system for themselves, just as a monarchy. Ask yourself; how often do elected officials speak in terms of fear, concern and uncertainty? Blaming one another is another tactic used to maintain a state of fear with Americans. We are being duped by a class of individuals (elected officials) and they have played off of the apathy, frustrations and fear by the Faithful Majority. It is not the eventual sacrifices when necessary entitlement programs are changed, the Faithful Majority have only to fear the politicians who maintain the political status quo of *Politics As Usual*. It is time for the politicians to live in a state of fear or choose to change the abuses of power and make right the entitlements that are now wrongly designed and structured for current times and needs.

large. Do they know the *true interests* of the American people? They do not live among us. They hear mostly from the media, polls, special interest lobbyists, information second hand from constituents through young, impressionable staff members. This is why there have been changes made by the electorate during the last two national elections. How much longer will we deny the truths and wisdom of our Founders?

Some Additional Thoughts on Monarchy and Hereditary Succession - Of Status Quo and Their Illusions of Power (1995)

This section contains some additional thoughts on the revision, adaptation and updates by the Author, based upon the segment from Common Sense, entitled Of the Monarchy and Hereditary Succession.

The designs and systems of American government have stood the test of time and abuses of humanity. *It is wholly owing to the constitution of the people and not to the constitution of the government* that America has prospered. The plan for the prosperous existence of society and government already exist within American government. During the last thirty years, amidst the wonderful achievements of equal rights for all Americans, the struggles and battles have left scars and wounds that have not yet healed. While, the struggles have been necessary, worthwhile and made a difference for America's future the dissension and growing diversity heightened and caused most Americans to stray from what it truly means to be an American. The *Faithful Majority* have set aside their responsibility in America's plan and her destiny. The Founders greatest fears of government have fallen prey to the worse side of human nature. Generally, the participants of *Politics As Usual* have ignored the wisdom, dignity, values and character necessary to work America's plan.

The formation of political parties was probably one of the few issues never considered by the Founders. Yet, with only a little experience of political parties, George Washington spoke in his farewell address in 1796 with regard to the *"spirit of the Party"*. His prophetic message very clearly describes the *"...disorders and miseries – the common and continual mischief of the spirit of Party."* Washington warns *"...to make it the interest and duty of a wise people to discourage and restrain it."*

To the *spirit of Party*, now *Politics As Usual* has attempted to make us believe government can be all things to all people. In this attempt, which is a miserable failure, the character of good and honorable people is questioned because of their promises that have created high expectations that actually end up in broken promises. Politicians have attempted to comply with the wishes of society and in the process have fallen prey to their egos and temptations of power in government. How can the People remain so distant from this degree of common sense?[34]

Now we understand the real genius of the Founding Fathers. They created three branches of government and a system of checks and balances on each branch of government and frequent elections. The Founders understood the nature of humanity and the paradoxes associated with the tendencies of human nature, the growth and changing of society's needs and the necessity of government for GENERAL security and welfare. They knew that freedom required flexibility for the individual and the individual's desires of the ego needed proper checks and balances to protect society from passionate extremes. They continually supported their ideals and structure of government by seeking to motivate and

---

34 Now we know why. Almost 50% of the People do not pay income tax and some 45% of households receive some form of federal subsidy. The People have become enslaved to the entitlements, just as Jefferson, Paine and Washington predicted. The elected officials are simply taking advantage of the People, for their selfish benefit and all who are involved in the Politics As Usual system, remain supportive and encourage the elected to continue doing what they do because all within the system reap vast rewards – always at the expense of the People, the Faithful Majority, who pay income tax. People lose perspective of the common good when 50% no longer pay income tax and more than 45% of the households receive federal subsidies? Who in political leadership will have the courage to address this imbalance of entitlements and put America back on track for great nation status versus just becoming another European type society?

inspire the electors to exercise their power to vote. As Paine wrote,

> ...*that the elected might never form to themselves an interest separate from the electors, prudence will point out the propriety of having elections often: because as the elected might by that means return and mix again with the general body of the electors in a few months, their fidelity to the public will be secured by the prudent reflection of not making a rod* (a badge of office, authority or power) *for themselves. And as this frequent interchange will establish a common interest with every part of the community, they will mutually and naturally support each other, and on this depends the strength of government, and the happiness of the governed.*

Paine envisioned the workings of a small community. He thought it could be expanded and work as easily throughout the eastern seaboard of America. The previous passage speaks of the good things that happen when good people get together and those people are accountable to the electors.[35]

---

35   An interesting twist to the Internet and various applications like Facebook and other social media is the development of communities of common interests. At the same time, the transparency of the small community atmosphere can be a major influence on building character and developing sustainable community values. This is very similar to the Pre-Revolution Colonies. The colonists were separated by distance and communication and they lived and worked in communities of special interests. When it came time to create the United States, each of these communities found the leadership to represent them in the discourse for creating the U.S. government. How might the Internet bring forth authentic leaders from the various communities of interest and establish an American discourse for common sense solutions to today's political and government issues?

All these considerations bring me to ponder upon the possibility of the workings of divine providence by God to bring together 55 men in 1787 of such different people, opinions, agendas and objectives. How did the Founders express their beliefs about God's divine providence in the formation of America?

The Constitutional Convention had been stalled until Benjamin Franklin made this call to prayer on June 28, 1787. This turning point was recorded by

Alexis De Tocqueville supported the designs of America's representative democracy with the following passage. Tocqueville was most observant of society in general, the political process, private lives and behaviors of the American people within fifty years of achieving independence. His Democracy in America (1835) can be viewed as an early publication on sociology and political science. His insights are as valid today, as then.

>...*The plan was a wise one. The general affairs of a country engaged the attention only of leading politicians, who assemble from time to time in the same places; and as they often lose sight of each other afterwards, no lasting ties are established between them. But if the object be to have the local affairs of a district conducted by the men who reside there, the same persons are always in contact, and they are, in a manner, forced to be acquainted and to adapt themselves to one another.*[36]

American government creates several paradoxes. The first and the biggest paradox is the Constitution of the United States of

---

James Madison of Franklin's call to prayer:

And have we forgotten that powerful Friend? Or do we imagine that we no longer need His assistance? I have lived, sir, a long time and the longer I live the more convincing proofs I see of this truth: that God governs in the affairs of men. And if a sparrow cannot fall to the ground without his notice, is it probable that an empire can rise without His aid? We have been assured, sir, in the sacred writings that 'except the Lord build the house, they labor in vain that build it.' I firmly believe this and I also believe that without His concurring aid, we shall succeed in this political building no better than the builders of Babel.

36   The intent of the Federal political structure is clear – *to assemble from time to time*, yet Federal elected officials now spend the majority of their time together, which means that *they adapt themselves to one another*, as Tocqueville writes. The difference between the local elected and Federal elected is the local have to face their constituents day-in and day-out and are required by law to maintain a balanced budget. The Federal elected no longer have to face their constituents regularly and when they do it is done through a staff member and the biggest difference, the Federal elected do not have to balance the budget. This has to change.

America. While it is simply written, human nature wants to achieve the promises of the Constitution. In the attempt to accomplish these promises, the intended simplicity of government has grown immensely in the attempt to deal with the complexities of society. All humans are social creatures. This includes all the people in Washington. We seek companionship and relationship for personal needs and desires. We network with one another for additional resources and establish strategic alliances to benefit our self-interests and those interests within our network. We enjoy these freedoms secured by the First Amendment – to establish these relationships. Then when we consider one of our fastest developing technologies is in the arena of telecommunications, we can now associate and maintain lasting ties even if those within our network live in every nook and cranny in the world.[37]

Secondly, the people in Washington are *forced to be acquainted [with] and to adapt themselves to one another.* Their longevity in Washington and continuous contact with one another has led to them adapting themselves to one another out of their fears, political affiliations and ego survival. They learn to prefer their Washington political environment because when they return to their communities, they must look upon the faces of the people and hear the problems that have been created by the political pandering and excessive legislation. Politicians measure their success by the amount of legislation they create or degree of

---

37 Obviously, as the Author, I enjoy reading my thoughts from 1995 and being in awe of the advances in technology, and yet disappointed in how *Politics As Usual* has only become more complex and frustrating. I began using the Internet in January 1995, when one had to use code to surf. It was within a few months that Mosaic came online and made it easier to surf. It was an interesting time and I have other articles about how the internet compared to the explosion of printed communications and letter writing during the Revolution and how the rapid expansion of the Internet led to a similar explosion in communications and sharing of ideas and concepts. The early days of the Internet were most interesting as people were exploring the possibilities with one another. I've got moments in time when I was communicating with individuals who could envision how these possibilities would manifest into businesses. A couple of them became major online leaders and known billionaires, today. Yes, there are many times when I've reflected upon those times and wish I had bought their stock, back then.

influence and power they have on new legislation and various positions on committees, and of course, some committees carry more influence than others. They even treat one another the way they treat the common People.

Otherwise, there is no measurement of their success except how much money they return to their constituents. Why not just leave the money in the communities in the first place? Why funnel it through the multiple layers of middlemen in Washington? They measure themselves by their presumed power or influence they have over each other. They do not trust one another and they are constantly negotiating, making trades and creating pork barrel legislation. And, if one doesn't play the game as it is designed, they do not get to enjoy the spoils that the system so generously bestows upon those of weakest character and values.[38] All in a grand illusion of cooperation. If they could not politically kill off or remove someone during their term in office, they release all their frustrations and angers on one another by means of undignified, blaming, fear-generating campaigns of tired and empty promises that they have no intention of ever achieving. *Politics As Usual* has lost any sense of statesmanship and the character and values of any politician has to be questioned as their integrity has been forgotten, long ago.

Thirdly, *We, the People* enjoy our freedom to not worry about the affairs of state as a matter of our daily lives, yet we are the ultimate authority. We have the freedom to vote and yet we have lost sight of the real power of our individual vote. We have become disinterested owners, leaving management to their own devices and with too much authority. Not unlike the professional athlete who

---

38 Numerous legislators can be named here. They have, long ago, sold their souls to the *Politics As Usual* devil. They are recognized by their influential positions on select committees and titles – more because of their length of time in office, not for their merit and not for their leadership. The shame they must feel when they are caught in a lie or obvious wrong-doing. Sadly, the only ones the public knows about are those that the influential elected status quo wants to remove from the system. It takes courage to want to be in that insidious environment. Many enter with dreams and hope to make change and few exit with those dreams and hopes intact. Most are assimilated into the system, like individuals are assimilated by the Borg.

makes a significant amount of money, gives another individual control over the money, only to return at some future point to find out the money has been squandered and stolen from right under their nose.

By the design of government, we have been trained to expect duly elected representatives will watch over and carry out their duty regarding the affairs of state – and so, doing that in the grace of God and as a servant to all Americans. Our faith in this system allows the *Faithful Majority* to concentrate on their self-interests and enhance the opportunities for all Americans. While in the pursuits of our self-interests, our apathy has allowed too many elected and unelected representatives to gain direct influence on the affairs of state. The people of America do not know who the unelected representatives are and these unelected have little care or concern for being a servant to the people of America. They care only for their own self-interests, as they design their jobs for maximum benefit and expense to the American People.

Fourthly, the multitude of lifestyle choices provided society has been affected by real American ingenuity and innovation. Entrepreneurs, executives and professionals are always learning to adapt and find the loopholes in compliance of the ever-growing complexity of laws, new legislation and bureaucratic regulations. This *American Spirit* continues to create opportunities and jobs, yet *Politics As Usual* is a democratic tyrant, continually expanding the people's dependency on government. The pendulum has swung too far to government and it is time for it to swing back to society and free enterprise.[39]

---

39 What more do we need to witness to understand the tyranny of the punisher? Businesses are not hiring as they have in the past when coming out of a recession. Uncertainty pervades business discussions, not only due to *Politics As Usual,* but also due to the rapid shift in the competitive business environment. So, not all is to blame on the lack of leadership by politicians. The Faithful Majority needs to awaken fully to the excesses and abuses of the political and bureaucratic systems while, at the same time, deciding to move forward with their businesses and actions that will help put America back to work.

During this economic crisis, private and public jobs have been cut and many of these are unlikely to return because of organization's ability to leverage

And lastly, the mass media can no longer deliver an accurate, educated message to the people. Sound-bites and slanderous advertising are without justice for the electorate seeking to know a political candidate and their personal agenda. The freedom in the growth of talk radio, talk television and on-line computer systems has allowed us to deliver a broader, more interactive message, but it, too, is limited by the peoples' lack of understanding of our American heritage and the Founders' wisdom, principles and values that created the most perfect system of government in the history of the world.

In the height of the Industrial Revolution, politicians were the pawns of free-enterprise to utilize government as a vehicle of continued growth and expansion. The politicians and bureaucrats resented their position as pawns to free-enterprise. Over the past sixty years, these political pawns have gained unimaginable powers over businesses. While business has always been a willing participant in the political process, even the captains of industry are not without concern. Politicians can command campaign contributions from opposing special interests on almost every issue. Most contributors give to both Republican and Democratic candidates. Business calls it *"Good Business"*, while the politicians laugh all the way to the bank. Who is manipulating whom?

THOUGHTS ON THE PRESENT STATE OF AMERICAN AFFAIRS (1995)

Introduction (1995)

This could be entitled *The Educating of Alan* (Author). The original segment from <u>Common Sense</u> entitled *Thoughts on the Present State of American Affairs* kept calling to me. As I read and re-read it, I continued substituting current-day events. Thomas Paine, two hundred and twenty years ago, made more sense to me than most

---

technology and some jobs are just not necessary any more. Much like the downsizings and reduction-in-force in the mid 1980s – many of the jobs cut had no reason to be refilled, even when economic conditions improved and turned around.

elected leaders and experts, who are enmeshed in today's *Politics As Usual*. The Founders' writings, thinking and discourse on liberty, government and society then, make a lot of sense now, because the Founders truly lived without their freedom and they risked their lives to gain that freedom. They had to be sure of themselves and what they were doing. They could not escape from their mistakes or they risked losing all that had been personally gained and some did lose it all for the stand they took. From their process of intense, person-to-person discourse, they created the United States, a simple and as near perfect government structure as can ever be achieved. At the same time, the Founders had a realistic understanding of humanity and society, and of the relationship and conflicts between government and society.

It is this near perfect simplicity and two hundred years of blessing the sacredness of the values and principles put forth in the Constitution and the Bill of Rights, which has allowed us our freedom. Americans freedoms have been secured for so long, Americans have not generally needed to truthfully engage in a common person-to-person discourse of the roles of government and society. America's representative democracy has allowed the American people to leave this discourse up to our representatives. In the process, *We the People,* have had the freedoms and luxury to focus on our work, families, schools and communities, which is what has really been responsible for America's success. Yet, it is the very freedoms we have enjoyed that are now rapidly changing nearly every aspect of our lives. With new communication technologies, we have literally thrown ourselves together into the same room, figuratively speaking.[40]

---

40   That was thinking back in 1995 and now in 2012; it is truly amazing the connections people share and the accessibility to information available to anyone who has access to do a Google search engine. Such online social media has already been the downfall of several promising political careers. It is time to up the stakes. Why not set up watchdog styled websites or Facebook sites for each politician. People can upload their videos and share their comments about the politicians' speaking, actions and legislation activities. Make it transparent as to whom and from where they receive their contributions and how that influences their voting activities. A metric for how much the elected official costs the People and how much they save, by the legislation enacted. When this is fully set, then set up the same for the

The many issues facing America can only be resolved by society reclaiming its rights, and this will primarily be accomplished by the *Faithful Majority*. Americans must learn to cooperate. Otherwise, the alternatives will not end up as we want them. Amazingly, computer technology, once feared, it would turn us into a mass society, has in reality made us all individuals. We are now engaging in a similar process as that of our Founding Fathers, a person-to-person discourse on the roles of government and society.[41]

I believe others are learning the truths, principles and values of America's Founders all across the nation. Individuals are discovering writings of the Founding Fathers and they are reading and re-reading those multiple times and engaging in relevant discourse. Each time they do so, richer and more meaningful understandings of freedom and liberty are realized as the current American state of affairs are deliberated and transacted. Many of the *Faithful Majority* are beginning to understand the true nature of the Founders' lives, the impact they had in 1776 and the immense ramifications their simple actions have made on us and beyond. *We, the People* are also beginning to get a glimpse into ourselves personally and our roles in the matters facing America and the world. We are realizing more each day; we truly do make a difference. Our votes make a difference and it is our responsibility to know the history, so we can *cover the whole ground* as opposed to parroting the sound-bites of blaming politicians.

Bureaucrat executives. When activity can be measured, it can be managed and it will change, rapidly when an individual knows and understands why and how they are being measured. People will adopt the right actions, behavior, attitude and character when they know they are being watched.

41   In the early 1980s, the book Mega Trends predicted this social phenomenon with the chapter entitled *High Tech, High Touch*. It is absolutely amazing to not only to be a part of this trend and personally witness the changes and advancements in the applications of technology, but to have written about the way things were twenty years ago and envision various possibilities has truly humbled me. Developing my ability to think through a variety of business, social and political issues from my readings and research to living out this journey can only be described as a continual sense of awe of how the process plays for this confluence of society, government, politics, self-interests, organizations and business.

In this process of *Educating Ourselves* on the truths of American democracy, we begin to understand ourselves more clearly and our duty to continue the greatness of the American heritage. We each are called to our duty to our progeny. To pass on to them our failings is unacceptable. In reality, we are doing as the Founders did. We are taking our knowledge, experience and resources, entering into a discourse with our peers, testing our views and opinions, forming concrete ideals and declaring the way we want things to be for ourselves, our families and communities.

We know what the Founders' actions produced. It is now our time to stand upon their shoulders and produce for ourselves what we want in our lives. It is within our power. It is our right and duty to do so.

Common Sense Revisited is my attempt at bringing all Americans to the eternal flame of liberty. Many individuals in America today are doing their part. *Common Sense* made things happen once before. My hope is that *Common Sense Revisited* will play a part in making it happen once more.

Thoughts on the Present State of American Affairs – Adapted From Paine's Common Sense (1995)

> The following has been adapted and updated by the Author from the original Thoughts on the Present State of American Affairs, by Thomas Paine in 1776.

In the following pages, I offer nothing more than simple facts, plain arguments, and common sense. I have no prior requests of the reader, than that they will set aside their prejudice and personal bias. The reader should think of their personal experience and understanding of the founding truths, principles, and values of America and the United States Constitution and Bill of Rights. The reader should permit their reason, common sense and their feelings to determine for themselves: that they will put on, or rather that they will not put off, the true character of the American People, and generously enlarge their views beyond the present day and their personal special interests.

Volumes have been written and thousands of hours of television and radio programming have aired, along with tens of thousands of meetings, seminars, conferences, government-funded studies, polls, speeches, discussions, opposing opinions and debates on the issues, problems and struggles faced in America. People of all lifestyles, ideologies; social, economic and political status have embarked on the many different controversies from different motives, and with various designs. Yet, there remains general discontent and skepticism with elected representatives to truly address the issues of government's waste, abuse, inefficiencies, entitlements, special privileges and gridlock. The time for common sense and reason by bold, courageous, authentic leaders is now. Political rhetoric, disrespectful, undignified mudslinging, blaming and positioning for reelection is no longer acceptable. Most of this has proven ineffectual for the People, and the period of debate is closed. True wisdom and decisive action as the last resource decide the contest; ever growing government bureaucracies and the gridlock of *Politics As Usual* was the choice of Congress and the Executive Office, and the American electorate has answered the challenge.

As with America's 1776 Revolution and subsequent birth of the United States, the sun once again shines on a cause of great worth. This is not the sole affair of a City, a County, a State, or just the federal government; but of all America. These are not just the concerns of a day, a year, or a single generation; all future generations are involved absolutely in the process, and will be more or less affected even to the end of time by the proceedings now. History has taught us that from the wisdom and actions by America's Founders, Americans have achieved a prosperity and standard of living beyond any conventional wisdom of 200 years or even 30 years ago. Now is the time for the re-seeding of American dignity, respect, unity, cooperation, character, values, faith, and honor. Unprecedented, yet the direction is clear and the actions necessary must reach across and unite America's diverse communities and cultures. The smallest fracture now will be like a name engraved with the point of a pin on the tender rind of a young oak; the wound would enlarge with the tree, and posterity will read it in full grown characters.

Only the wisdom of true leadership, the likes of which birthed America – will be accepted – that which will renew the *American Spirit* and empower individuals to be the best they can be. No longer will political side-stepping, blaming rhetoric stand up to the will of the electorate. It is the obligation and responsibility of all elected officials to put *Politics As Usual* to the test of reason and common sense; to be bold and make the tough decisions that inspire Americans to expand their sense of personal responsibility and take necessary actions to play a role in the improvement of America's future and set aside personal self-interests for our progeny. It is the obligation and personal responsibility of all Americans to set aside special interests, in the name of social causes which strengthen the political and bureaucratic grip on all Americans. The electorate must demand that elected officials put all government programs to the test of reason and common sense and the subsequent changes put forth must receive the acceptance of the majority of the electorate.

The elections of November 1994, once again, demonstrated a mandate for change. Those elected must be bold in accepting the challenge for making the changes or the electorate will make more sweeping changes in future elections. Americans want a revolution, a renewal of wisdom that will lead to a re-thinking of the way government works. Further gridlock and lack of action regarding tough decisions may result in the second *American Revolution*. The Republicans and Democrats risk being left behind. It has happened before.[42]

In making reference to recent elections, this is a reminder to all elected that the real power remains in the decision of the electorate. The elected have the duty and the opportunity to establish a new era for America and the world. The 90's can come to be known for the time that the truths of democratic thinking arose from the ashes of apathy, and the *Faithful Majority*, who believe in the basic

---

42 This was written by the Author in 1995 and remains true in 2012. Seventeen years later, the politicians remain in gridlock and resist making necessary changes, while it is obvious the rapid changes occurring throughout America and the world.

freedoms and ideals of America, demanded the elected to return to reason, courage, dignity and determination. The elected should make necessary changes in campaigning. They should, therefore, be relentless and risk the loss of favor and monies of the special interests and do what is right – do what feels right in their heart and do what is right for all future progeny. Only honorable duty should receive acclaim. Selfishness will also be easily recognized and despised.[43]

After the recent elections, much is being said about the advantages of the Republicans and Democrats reconciling their differences and finding the means to work together, cooperate and compromise. This could be like a dream which quickly passes away and leaves us as we were. It is just right that we should examine the possibilities of the continued gridlock, and inquire into some of the many material injuries which private Americans will sustain now and in the future by a burdensome and growing government (this includes every city, municipality, regional, county and state government).[44]

Will the elected set aside the *spirit of the Party*, demonstrate the courage and cooperate by standing within the wisdom of America's Founders? When will they be willing to stand up to the challenge of being the architects of a strategy which will inspire and empower all Americans to pursue a new level of excellence for the *American Dream*? Or will the elected once again speak the political rhetoric, take the political party side-of-the-aisle and platforms, remain in servitude to the special interests and leave America as it has been or worse?[45] Americans have the constitutional right to question,

---

43 Sadly, this is not the result of the 1990s. It has been just more of the same, while the deficit and debt have exploded in size. Sure, there are those politicians who will point the finger toward the Great Recession and the Republicans, as the cause for the gridlock, but all are responsible for the challenges America faces in 2012 and beyond. All are responsible for the accelerating downward spiral toward outcomes no one wants to imagine. When will the authentic, courageous leaders emerge to make things right again, for the People?

44 The good news from the Great Recession of 2008 is that government payrolls have shrank a little bit, but not enough.

45 It has gotten much worse. The Federal Deficit and Debt have tripled in size

inquire and examine the problems and issues now faced by the elected and demand the truths of the effective and the ineffective results produced by government's programs and bureaucratic agencies.

By referring this matter from the arguments and dissention of political parties to unity, a new era of politics is struck. A new method of thinking arises. All plans, proposals and legislation prior to these times, events and revelations of the early 1990's, i.e. the stalemated and stagnated legislature and executive branch, the gross negligence and abuse of special congressional privileges, the excessive influence of special interests, the massive costs of entitlements, interest on the national debt, voter ingratiation with pork barrel-promises and the slow, antiquated bureaucratic systems (which may have seemed proper and appropriate then are now untouchable institutions of shame because of tradition) are superseded. No sacred-cow escapes the grasp of review, true reform and/or removal.

America stands as the world's leader and defender of all human rights to life, liberty and the pursuit of happiness. In Government's valiant attempt to fulfill these rights for every human being and attempts to legislate compassion, the cure has become punishing and deadlier than the disease. Government programs addressing children, the poor, the sick, the elderly and all others who are deemed disadvantaged have fallen far short of expectations and the typical solution of ineffective elected leaders is to double down with more money, which only grows the bureaucracy of privileged executives beyond reproach or even measurement to determine their effectiveness. The administrative functions of these programs have become so ingrained into society that what might have been a temporary assistance program now has existed through several generations of a single family. There are now individuals who demand, by their birthright, that they are entitled. Maybe it was the right thing in the past, but now the questions must be asked; "What is the role of government? What is the role of society? Is society now better equipped to deal with these issues? Who believes that

---

since Common Sense Revisited was first written. From $4 Trillion in debt and $200 Billion deficit in 1995 to $14 Trillion in debt and over $1 Trillion deficit in 2012.

government is the rightful one to deal with issues and matters of the home? Society's compassionate caring through government, has taken many prisoners in the war on poverty – by default, government programs have become unemotional and inefficient caretakers.

Whatever legislation on the many issues was advanced by either the Republicans or the Democrats it has ended at one and the same point. Higher taxes, growing government, exploding entitlements and special privileges for all Congressional Members has only ingrained *Politics As Usual* as America's true political process. This process has been watched over by the informed insiders and the self-serving, deal making and pork barreling of the status quo and special interests. The only difference between the Republicans and Democrats has been the method of speaking and blaming about it. Each has proposed what has sounded good at the time and they attack each other when one has a slip of the tongue or tells the truth. They take that advantage in the hopes of burying an opponent with blame and to create fear in the voter, under enough political mud and the rules of the House and Senate. They exist in a culture of their own. These players of politics sink the real issues into the quagmire of Capitol Hill with their incessant debates and the misuse of the rhetoric of democracy. Either on purpose or by default, Congress has allowed *Politics As Usual* to remain. Both political parties have failed and yet both continue to speak to the American People, speaking similar concepts from different platforms. They sling mud at opponents to avoid the issues. They say what the polls have told them that Americans want to hear in the hopes of raising their percentages on a popularity poll. Who do the pollsters really ask? The politicians are out of touch. Long lost is the call to duty and only reside in Washington for brief periods of time. Elected officials no longer live amongst their constituents. They watch polls too much and actually hope that the electorate will fade away between elections, stay apathetic and remain uninformed and undereducated to the wisdom and common sense that founded this great nation, and has time and again enriched America. *We, the People* have allowed *Politics As Usual* too much power. The result is the enslavement of the Faithful Majority.

It is the electorate's apathy between elections and then casting undereducated and uninformed votes which is America's weakness, and we have allowed the politicians, bureaucrats and lobbyists to speak endlessly and argue over the issues and without actions to solve the problems and challenges of America. Still, they return to their only solution; to get themselves or their party leaders re-elected and by design or default, make government bigger and more complex. By what declared right in the Constitution of the United States have politicians and bureaucrats (all who work for the People and are on the public's payroll) come to feel entitled as that of a privileged class of their own. *Politics As Usual* has failed and the electorate must now exhibit its influence and exercise its Constitutional rights, which is where the real power exists.

Politicians are primarily insulated and removed from having to live with the errors of their judgments because of their special congressional privileges. They are neither fiscally accountable nor responsible to the American people for the debacles of their legislation and creation of bureaucratic behemoths. Yet, every private American must remain fiscally accountable and responsible to the government. In fact, private Americans now work one third (1/3rd) of their employable year to support the massive government, bureaucracies and entitlements. This will only grow with time, if left unchecked and not changed.[46] It is absolutely unconstitutional for Americans to be indentured slaves to government and the entitlements of a politician's newest and grander *New Deal* / *Great Society*. Will the politicians eventually come face to face with the reality of their character flaws and lack of courage? Will they know that for the remainder of their lives, and know in their hearts that their fears and lack of courage to offend a minority, special interest or center of influence may determine a child's faith and hope of living the *American Dream*? The obvious choice is clear, but when the time comes, will the elected stand up for the choice they know is right?

Without question, America has flourished under the influence, decisions and actions by former elected leaders. *Politics As Usual* has gotten us to where we are, say some. So, why change? It can be said

---

46 The percentage of people who do not pay income tax has risen from 23% in 1962 to 49.5% in 2009. Source: 2012 Index of Dependence on Government. This establishes an alarming trend when deficits and debts are exploding, the country is in a recession and entitlement costs are likewise exploding. +

that the same is necessary for America's future happiness, and will always have the same effect. Nothing can be more misleading than this kind of argument. We may as well assert that because a child has thrived upon milk, that they are never to have meat or vegetables, or that the first twenty years of our lives are to become a precedent for the next twenty. But even this is admitting more than is true. I answer whole-heartedly that America would have flourished as much, and probably much more had not the tremendous entitlements of special interest legislation, congressional special privileges, regulations and the behemoth bureaucracies entrenched today had never been enacted. America and the American people have been enriched beyond any conventional wisdom. Americans and America's founding principles and values have proven themselves with the passage of time and under all conditions, primarily by the actions of private individuals and private enterprise, not by new and improved, burdensome government programs.

During the entire history of America, even from its founding, there have been special interests, diversity of opinions and ideologies, diversity of cultures and abuse of power, taxation abuses and special privileges. What we see in government today has occurred before. It has been resolved before. This is the firm and flexible nature of the government structure established by America's Founders. America's government structure has proven itself flexible and strong because of the endearment of the Constitution and Bill of Rights by all Americans seeking the blessings of life, liberty and the pursuit of happiness. Each time America has faced similar issues and challenges; these have been met and overcome, always making America better and stronger. This has happened only by decisive leadership. Now is the time for private Americans to renew that the United States Constitution is of the people, not of the government. Now is the time to open the door and welcome the leadership which will step away from *Politics As Usual* and be truthful to the electorate and deliberate in their actions.

America's birth was based also upon the freedoms of enterprise, and America today thrives on individual American innovation and determination of millions of individuals to enrich themselves, their families, their businesses and their communities.

The opportunities of enterprise in the rapidly expanding information age are so abundant and vast that an individual today can create a personal legacy only dreamed of or imagined by history's feudal lords, kings and tyrants. Today's captains of industry and informational age are enriching the lives of millions in every corner of the world and being richly rewarded for their efforts. No nation can thrive by the designs of big government. Free enterprise demands effective and limited government.

It is time for *Politics As Usual* to remove bureaucracy's choking grasp on productive Americans.[47] Many other nations of the world are rapidly learning to thrive upon the principles and values proven by Americans. They have embraced democratic thinking, natural reason, common sense, free enterprise, innovation and entrepreneurship, and they are challenging every American's future.

The American people have been the unquestionable leaders in entrepreneurship and innovation. The American entrepreneurial spirit thrives in every corner of the United States, yet government regulations continue to burden this spirit. Free enterprise is the engine for economic growth, job growth and expansion of opportunities. Entrepreneurs always find the ways and means to pursue a dream, open doors of opportunity and to make things happen. We should not allow ourselves to discover what would be the consequences of continually burdening the very engine that builds jobs with government regulations and taxes. Burdensome bureaucracies do not meet the test of reason and common sense.

But *Politics As Usual*, new legislation and the government bureaucracy have protected and enhanced the individual's rights and business opportunities, some say. The fact that the elected representatives have built up government, which has benefited us has some truth, and that the government stands ready to defend any American's rights anywhere in the world is absolutely true. America's generosity reaches around the world for the motives of

---

47   Amazing how the economic crisis of 2008 would encourage politicians and bureaucrats to quickly pursue the expansion of their self-centered powers versus doing what is right for the People. Thus, proving the wisdom of Paine on the Patron or the Punisher – politicians and bureaucrats only seek to punish those they blame for being the cause. The end result, they punish all the People, especially those individuals they espouse to protect.

human rights, security and commerce. Yet, the world has changed and remaining with the status quo may severely limit America's future in or compared with world competition.

We have been long led away by old prejudices and have made necessary sacrifices to correct the injustices of past transgressions in America's history of oppression of human rights and inequality. Social government programs enacted during times of crisis – nationwide economic depression, assistance to the poor and the elderly, civil rights and equal rights have long been touted by politicians and special interests as proof of their watching out for the interests of the poor, under-privileged and middle class. The electorate supported these programs, but has now for too long tolerated, in the name of compassion, the *New Deals and The Great Society*, which have passed their prime. These programs have existed too long, without considering the long-term effect on posterity. The pandering influence of *Politics As Usual* fears to question or change these programs. These programs have become entitlements and any politician courageous enough to address the real issues is immediately attacked and all the other politicians swoop in for the kill by saying, *"I would not touch Social Security or Medicare."*[48] Their cowardice and selfishness is only for the preservation or reinstatement of their political party's majority and not the general welfare of all Americans. *Politics As Usual* and Society's short-term view and selfishness will lay ruin on posterity. Let their names be

---

48 *Common Sense Revisited* was originally published in 1995, to demonstrate the similarities of the current times to how power and politics worked even 220 years ago, when Thomas Paine first published Common Sense. Now, in 2012, how many attacks have there been and will be on Paul Ryan for his attempts to address the financial solvency of Medicare? The Faithful Majority know changes must be made to entitlement programs and some will have to sacrifice more than others. The key ingredient missing in these debates are the authentic leaders who will call upon the Faithful Majority to lead other politicians and this nation through this complex process. And, evoking God's divine providence as Franklin did at the Constitution Convention should be done today, as well. What damage can it do? Why would anyone deny the hand of God if all the various factions and special interests were to somehow come together and seek the common ground of common sense and reason? In the end, this Author is convinced there will be some similar story as Franklin's in how the stalemate was broken in 1787.

duly recorded and placed upon the rolls for America's progeny to rebuke and scorn the politician's existence.

These programs have not always provided the expected benefits to those individuals truly in need and have often, in reality, provided benefits to many not in need. The growing numbers of the poor and their miseries make it clear the programs have not met expectations. Many individuals have played with and abused the system and are unworthy of the benefits they are receiving or the system needs to be revamped to consider the personal development needs and skills training needs of the individual.

Bureaucrats also play their own games of politics, wasting the public's money and continuing to grow huge political machines, in spite of the fact they have few successful results to show for their efforts after billions and trillions of dollars spent. We must acknowledge these failures, throw off the ineffective programs and create able bodied individuals, who are independent of government programs and allow them to become productive members of society. It is time to get the job done. No *Grand New Deals* are needed.[49]

Some will say, but government should continue these programs with more money and the disadvantaged just need more time. Then the true nature of *Politics As Usual* is clear. The intention is not compassion, but to be an oppressive caretaker and seek the power and influence of a tyrant over the weakened minds of the

---

[49] As the Author, I can toss out various ideas. Some have been deeply thought through while others are simply a fresh idea with only minimal thinking time. This is one of those fresh ideas, for me. I'm sure others have considered this possibility before. Possibly one grand deal might work.

Create a Super Bureaucracy that acts like a vulture venture group, whose sole purpose and funding is based upon *taking over* the ineffective and inefficient bureaucracies. With each take over, the objectives would be clearly stated that a certain percentage of savings must be realized and metrics be put into place that required for a percentage of funding that had to find its way into the actual hands of those receiving the benefits. Additionally, metrics of service and satisfaction by the beneficiaries must be measured to be the check and balance on the bureaucracy. The hopes for this Super Bureaucracy would be to lessen the smothering burdens, reduce costs and motivate other bureaucracies to get their act in line or be absorbed.

disadvantaged. In reality, this practice has entrapped able-bodied individuals in demeaning lifestyles. Bureaucrats for the disadvantaged have been known to even take away privileges from those individuals who attempted to demonstrate some degree of initiative and innovation to break free of being a burden on society.[50]

Acceptance and forgiveness must replace blame and accusation. These regulations and programs deserve some degree of fanfare and acclaim. Yet, it is time for these programs to demonstrate exceptional success at bringing the disadvantaged into productive roles in society. Some elected officials and special interests continually exclaim that racism and inequalities are rampant in society. They do so for motives of political selfishness and additional funding, as opposed to promoting real care and concern, responsibility and self-reliance for others.

Individuals who connect themselves with these leaders and special interests remain dependent on tired ideals and past miseries. An individual must break free from those thoughts that bind one's dignity, self-respect, self-reliance and personal responsibility. Everyone must put themselves to the test. They must challenge themselves to take responsibility...to relinquish the role of victim or blaming the current generation for past transgressions by prior generations for the cause of limitations on their current situations in life. Many others have overcome. They should be the examples and the mentors, not the leaders who continue to yell that the sky is falling.

Some amount of failure is certain. Forgetting the failures, but not the lessons is a necessity. Persistence strengthens character and character is always acknowledged and rewarded. God is the giver of life and it is true that all people are created equal. Yet, God's special gift to humanity has been our ability to make choices. An

---

50 If the recipients of benefits get a job, they are limited to how much they can make, so ambition is capped. Imagine the life of an individual who has no ambition. This is not much better than the institutionalization of mentally challenged people in the 1950s. These are systems designed to entrap and enslave people for the bureaucrats benefit. Why can't these entitlement programs design incentives that inspire people as so many non-profit organizations are doing today, like Goodwill Industries?

individual's existence, as a member of society, demands that each and every individual must earn their right to life, liberty and the pursuit of happiness. There is no self-esteem to be gained without some personal strife and struggle. This is just part of life. The rewards are abundant for those who pursue American liberties, and freedom is the preferred choice in America.

Temporary needs of assistance are understood and compassionately given by society. The overlooked tolerances of government assisting disadvantaged individuals and even generations of the same family for long periods of time is not understood by a society that was founded on values of hard work, smart-work and genuine effort. Society is willing to provide long-term assistance to the individual who is totally incapacitated and without family, friends, church or community. Throughout the history of the world, all attempts by governments to be the *equalizer* (redistribute the wealth) have failed. These have all been for the designs of making one individual all powerful, thus making those punishers, tyrants and dictators.

Now, in these times of change and chaos, the means to accomplish the immense tasks for reforming government cannot be accomplished with the out-of-date concepts or the demeaning and dependency-generating policies of government programs.[51] Selfish, bureaucratic motives and misappropriation of resources will no longer be tolerated. Individuals capable of contributing to society must do so just as the majority of Americans. Private corporations have learned to cut out the middleman and large chunks of middle management. Likewise, it is time for government to follow the ways of private enterprise. The people's money should be accomplishing what it is truly intended for not paying for inefficient government systems and employees *hired for life*.

I challenge the warmest advocate for *Politics As Usual* to show any advantages of remaining with the current status quo. If these ways and means have been successful then why do we have more social workers today than ever in America history?[52] At the same

---

51 Reminder that this was written in 1995 and it is the same in 2012, only worse.

52 Why are there more people than ever not paying income tax and the numbers of people on food stamp programs are increasing at an alarming rate?

time, why are there are more poor individuals and disadvantaged than ever in American history? Billions of dollars have been spent on education. Why are test scores lower and dropout rates higher than ever before? Too many stories are being told of how government programs, unchecked and without any recourse to government bureaucrats have written policies and regulations that provide incentives *to potentially disadvantaged individuals* to appear ever more disadvantaged than they really are to just receive the Peoples' money. With more disadvantaged people, the bureaucrats show the necessity of growing the program by needing to hire more employees and increase the salaries of the bureaucrats. I repeat the challenge; the few advantages, if any, do not warrant the inefficiencies, huge costs and false imprisonment of individuals that, in reality, are capable of being productive. The solutions to the issues and problems being faced in America today do not reside in *Politics As Usual* and the outdated beliefs in government programs and bureaucratic organizations. Albert Einstein said,

> *"The world will not evolve past its current state of crisis by using the same thinking that created the situation."*

New alternatives and new concepts are required to bring all Americans into the new era. The design of open, democratic cooperation and collaboration, decisive leadership and a wise electorate working together will make the right choices. Productive strategies will emerge for a new American era to be brought forth. Its' time has come.

The injuries and disadvantages which we sustain by *Politics As Usual* are without number; and our duty to humanity at large, as well as to ourselves, instructs us to renounce the error of our leisurely, inactive, misinformed, non-voting and apathetic ways. Any submission to or dependence upon *Politics As Usual* tends directly to maintain the issues and problems which now exist. As freedom to life, liberty and the pursuit of happiness is the cornerstone of America's existence, then we must break from the bonds of our complacent and complicated ways of government. It is the true interest of all Americans to steer clear of being apathetic and dependent on tired political rhetoric and demand true American leadership.

Politics As Usual is too thickly planted with the status quo and political party leaders with the comforts of their *kingdoms* to trust them to bring forth revolutionary changes. Their actions have proven that they intend to be re-elected and they already are working to return or maintain their political party as the majority party. Politicians are blinded to the truths of power and the misuse of power. They miss opportunities to seize upon genuine actions which will insure the freedoms and liberties of the majority of Americans. Their blindness places the freedoms and liberties we have come to expect in jeopardy for future generations. Entitlement burdens must be resolved, yet the elected refuse to speak the truth, for fears of losing the next election. If changes are not made in the entitlements, bankruptcy is a possibility and their excess will lay ruin on posterity.[53] Advocates for *Politics As Usual*, then as always is the case, will be pleading for changes to be made and they will even say they tried before and each political party will blame the other. Everything that is right or reasonable pleads for revolutionary changes. The blood, sweat and tears of Americans, the weeping voice of nature cries, *"It is time to change and make things the way they should be."* Even the fact that the eventual results of changes are unknown, there is our American heritage and the many peaceful changes of political power to show sufficient proof that the *Faithful Majority* and the *American Spirit* will always triumph and prevail.

Apathetic Americans look somewhat lightly over the offenses of current events, while still hoping for the best and are apt to say, *"Relax, everything will turn out okay. It always has."* But examine the passions and feelings of the *Faithful Majority* and bring the performance of *Politics As Usual* to the touchstone of nature. Then tell me whether you can hereafter love, honor, and faithfully believe in those individuals who sustain that which has stagnated, stalemated and mortgaged your children's' future. If you remain apathetic and faithfully believe in the proponents of *Politics As Usual*, then you are only deceiving yourselves, and by your delay,

---

53   This cannot be emphasized enough. This was written in 1995 and in 2012, all debt and deficits have tripled or more and growing. More people pay no income tax. The revenue coming into government is significantly less than what is going out in costs. In any household, that spells bankruptcy, if continued for any length of time.

bringing ruin upon posterity. Your future allegiance to *Politics As Usual*, which deserves neither love nor honor, will be forced and unnatural. You will maintain your beliefs only because of your present conveniences. Your delays to vote for and be personally responsible for changes now will soon reveal issues and problems of immense magnitude, more wretched than what we see today. But if you say you can still pass over the issues and problems forced upon American society, then I ask if you can review the following list and truly believe all will be okay?

This is not a complete list of issues and problems facing America. That would take a huge book. Neither do the questions deal with the differing perceptions of what equal rights is suppose to be, because equal access to opportunity has been achieved for most all Americans. While racism, sexual abuse and child abuse exist, the many facets of these issues must be dealt with personally and responsibly. Neither government, nor the legal system can deal with every possible issue. This has been one of the underlying problems. Those receiving their equal rights in the last few decades have maybe expected things to be easier than they have. It has not been easy. And there have been some extremist, unethical and immoral individuals who have actually abused their rights by falsely accusing for personal selfish gain. They have been able to do so without penalty of retribution.

Government and Elected Leaders:

- Is there any part of your life not regulated by some government agency? Look again!

- Have you continued to pay more taxes and yet the problems and issues keep getting bigger?

- Do you know someone exploiting welfare and other government give-away programs?

- Do you ever wonder why so many people working for the government are just not getting the job done? Yet, bureaucracies continue to grow. Does it work that way in private enterprise?

- Why must there be so many regulations and new legislation that expands into volumes of books versus simplicity and transparency?

- Do you own a business and have you had an employee terrorize your business with threats of legal actions because the employee, a government employee and an attorney schemed a way of using unreasonable government regulations to extort money from your business? And you are almost at a place of feeling you cannot do anything about it.

- Has your business been threatened, unmercifully, by a government employee or agency, which refused to understand all the facts and issues? You are guilty, first – and then, you have to prove your innocence versus them proving your guilt.

- Why do elected leaders pander to the special interests and all their money, instead of passing true lobby and campaign reforms? Don't they already have the best of the best in benefits for the time they spend in service to the American people? How do they live with themselves, in life after politics, after they have enriched themselves in ways that for the general population and conventional wisdom would put most people in prison?

- Where are the authentic leaders, who are willing to fight and win the battle against *Politics As Usual?* When will they once again draw the line between government and society?

General Society Issues:

- Has your property been vandalized and the police say there is little they can do because they cannot abuse the suspects' rights?[54]

- Do you know someone falsely accused of sexual harassment, child abuse or racism? It is done for spite and the accuser faced no retribution. Once again, guilty until an extensive process to be proven innocent. There must be a way of finding out sooner that the accuser may be lying.

- Do you know of a destitute family or child, not receiving benefits? Then you read about scandal and losses of millions of dollars within a government program.

---

54 How about identify theft? Your identity is stolen, you know who did it and yet, the financial institution or police have no interest in pursuing because it is too difficult to prove guilt. How can such a system be constructed that the thieves are able to get away it what they do just because the companies can make those who pay their bills pay for their losses? And, then you get some new Federal bureaucratic program such as the credit card debt relief act that professes to protect the consumer, in reality, all the new regulations cause additional fees to be charged to the consumer. Where is the logic in this?

- Have the spoils of drugs upset and changed your way of life with your family or community? Yet, the drug dealers cannot be kept in jail.

- Have you heard about innocent children being gunned down in a drive-by shooting? Again, the murders cannot be apprehended or they get off scot-free?

- Have you been called to jury duty to hear a case where the plaintiff lost the case and did not have to pay the defendant for all his/her lost time and attorney's expenses? The accuser can be proven false without repercussions, yet the defendant has to pay even proven guilty, even when they may not be.

- Do you wonder if your children are receiving a proper education to prepare them for future competition?

Economy and Free Enterprise:

- Are you feeling insecure with all the changes in the economy, business and technology and wondering why American business is struggling to compete around the world?

- Are you on Social Security and willing to work, but the regulations penalizing you to do so?

- Do you want a raise in your income and the owner talks about how tight the profit margins are and how there is no certainty of the future?

- Have you inquired with the business owner regarding all the taxes, costs of preparing government forms and information profiles and the costs of hiring experts and professionals to deal with the mountains of government regulations? Now, do you understand who is getting money that could be coming to you? That's what is called a "ghost-tax". Because of all the regulations and taxes, businesses cannot increase wages to the people who make the business happen.

These questions are not inflaming or exaggerating matters, but rather seek to bring forth the feelings and sense of direction needed for us to engage into a discourse to resolve the issues and problems of society and government. We know this is possible because the Founding Fathers were able to come together and build a framework of understanding that led to the formation of the United States. If we do not, then we risk loss of our freedoms of life, liberty and the pursuit of happiness. I mean not to provoke protest or call for revenge, but to awaken us from fatal and apathetic slumbers. *We, the People* must determinately pursue some fixed strategy to bring a separation of government and society. It is not in the power of *Politics As Usual* to deal with and conquer society's problems. *Politics As Usual* is in reality conquering the *American Spirit* with ongoing strategies for delay and timidity. They are either intentional about this process or totally ignorant of the system at work around them. Sort of like the myth of the frog in a pot of boiling water. The frog will sit in the pan and die because the temperature changes over a period of time. Truth be told – a frog will jump out of the pot, yet politicians are willing to stay in the boiling water until they die. Most appear to do it for personal selfish gain versus a genuine calling to their duty of service to their country. Maybe the recent election has set the agenda. If this is so, let us make the sacrifices now. If the elected do not act, 1996 cannot be neglected by the electorate or America's future will sustain even greater misfortunes and our sacrifices will be much greater. There is no punishment deserving for the elected and the electorate for sacrificing this moment of truth, so precious and useful.[55]

It is foolish to reason that our Founding Fathers would approve of the current state of affairs. We can suppose the Founder's would fear America's freedoms and liberties could not endure the decisions and actions of *Politics As Usual* for very long. Even the most confident cannot think so. Even the most wise or outstanding political or management strategies cannot form the basis of a plan without major changes to current bureaucratic systems or political methods. Neither can they make unrealistic promises such as no one in America having to make some sacrifice. Maintaining status quo is now an unreasonable dream. All natural reason and common sense has been deserted, and no amount of political rhetoric or political positioning can return everything to the way it was. Insanity has been defined as the expectation that the outcome will be different by expending more effort, money and

---

55 SADLY – this is getting old by how many times the Author has repeated that word. The elected have only acted in ways that have worsened America's situation from 1995 to 2012 – and, the Faithful Majority has allowed this to happen. It cannot continue this way. The Founding Fathers designed and established a process for preserving what works and sustaining the American Spirit. Change is now an absolute for America to return to greatness.

vast resources on the same solutions, which have already been proven not to correct the problem.

As to government matters, it is not in the power of *Politics As Usual* to do the American people justice. The business of government has become too weighty, intricate and complicated to be managed with any tolerable degree of convenience, by powers so removed from the mainstream of society, and so very ignorant. A few career politicians hold new arriving politicians in a stranglehold. There cannot be career politicians. If the politicians and bureaucrats cannot live under the very rules, regulations, health plans and social security programs as they impose upon us, then they should not have the right to govern us. Their duty, as elected representatives and government employees, is to serve all Americans. In our apathy, we have forgotten that the electorate holds the power.

The Constitution describes most simply the broad areas of concern for government. *We, the People* are responsible to provide the discipline, and it has been too long since the electorate provided true discipline. But, there is something absurd in supposing all American People are to be perpetually cared for or shown special considerations through special interests, constantly generating new laws and bureaucratic structures, creating an insane amount of regulations, accompanied by its mountains of paperwork and excessive costs. In no instance has nature made the attempt at being an absolute provider and protector of all species and in no instance can it be found. Only man has attempted to do so and there have been many grand experiments. God does not even attempt to do such a thing. All attempts by humanity to create government to care for its entire people and make all people equal, has failed. Government can only assure the *Equality of Opportunity*. All of nature and all attempts by humanity have proven that all experiments of government to make *everyone equal* and redistribute the wealth so everyone has an equal amount leaves a nation in the ruin of mediocrity, food shortages, general helplessness and uninspired and de-spirited peoples. It is absolutely evident that government and society are different systems. Government to its Constitution and regulations that are simple and meet the test of reason and common sense: The American People to their rights to Life, Liberty and the pursuit of Happiness.

But how, some say, can change of such magnitude and proportion not create immense degrees of havoc, confusion and crisis for Americans and humanity around the world? I'll tell you, friend, it begins with our faith in God and then the faith in a nation of people existing with a two hundred and twenty year heritage of freedom and liberty. The spirit of the American People will sustain and will be the stabilizing factor during these changes. While changes in the operations of government occur, the actual daily activities of the American People will change very little. The *Faithful Majority* will maintain their personal activities regarding their work, families and community. Yet, there will be a renewal of energy within the people, the likes of which put a man on the moon, ended the fear of global nuclear war and slowed even reversed humanity's impact on the environment.

But, where, some say, is the leadership with the faith, courage, dedication, integrity, common sense, dignity and judgment to lead America through these times? Our leadership comes from the ordinary people, ready, willing and able to be *uncommon* in the face of *Politics As Usual.* This new leadership must leave behind outdated beliefs and prejudices and must reach across barriers once seen as impenetrable. Beliefs have changed in the past and for the betterment of humanity, such as with the cases of slavery, women without a vote and the *Berlin Wall.* Our nation has always survived and thrived. Our faith in constitutional rights, laws and faith in God have sustained us through times of great changes, crisis and times of quiet. Our faith allows for us to be complacent and apathetic during times of quiet and that same faith demands from us responsible, democratic actions in times of crisis and change. *Politics As Usual* should not maintain its power as long as the final say is totally within the rights and power of all American People.

A government of the people, by the people and for the people is a constitutional right - our natural right: and, when people seriously reflect on the precariousness of human affairs, they will become convinced, that it is infinitely wiser and safer to take their God-given right of choice and exercise their Constitutional freedoms by their actions and votes in a cool, educated, deliberate manner. We must act while the opportunities for necessary changes are in our power, rather than to trust such interesting and far-reaching events to time and chance and the stagnation of *Politics*

As Usual.

To allow for the continuation of *Politics As Usual*, in which all natural reason forbids us to have faith, is madness and folly. Every day exhausts the few remains of the faith in elected representatives. Can there be any reason to hope, that as the faith expires, our expectations will increase, or that we shall have more faith when we have ten times more issues and problems to face?

Can the staunch supporters of *Politics As Usual* truly justify the failure of the welfare state and its demeaning result on the *American Spirit?* The changes have begun. We saw many of those who created the current *Politics As Usual* retire and lose their bids for reelection because they saw what was to come and were blatantly out-of-step with mainstream America. A few changes in government bureaucracy and regulations are happening and beginning to be noticed. It is the duty of the *Faithful Majority* to see that these changes continue. The past injuries and entitlement burdens must not be placed upon posterity. Our children and their children's children had no choice in these matters. We must see that these burdens are removed and allow them, when their time comes, to choose their own destinies, just as it is our time to choose ours.

America has been blessed with leaders of compassion and feelings for good and wise purposes. They have distinguished America from the rest of the world. Many times in America's history, the Constitution and our freedoms could have disappeared - justice and our freedoms might have been eliminated from the earth, or only have a casual existence, were our leaders callous to their compassions. Yet, while robbers and murderers are often escaping unpunished, the American People are being enslaved by their own willingness to live within ever-increasing discomforts of burdensome rules and regulations. How can this be? A nation with such resources available as in our country and there still exists all the problems and issues. The ultimate responsibility then can only be with *We, the People.* We must discipline elected representatives and bureaucrats to control themselves and their spending. For this and many other reasons, the *Faithful Majority* have been provoked, demanding that justice be served with the voice of reason. *Politics As Usual* has been warned; the truths of America's democratic process will always, like Mother Nature, prevail. The power and the voice of the American People will see that justice is served and our freedoms shall appear as if they never had been in jeopardy.

All peoples that love humankind! You that dare oppose *Politics As Usual* stand forth! Every spot of our nation is overrun with problems. The ways of the world have changed. Unforeseen events have let loose freedom and capitalism around the world. Even the dissolved Soviet Union is attempting to embrace these freedoms, as well as other nations. A true leader sets a good example for others to follow. It is without question the time for dedicated actions and common sense judgments for necessary changes, and the demonstration of the integrity of the American people to be responsible and accountable to themselves and the world. How the American People address and resolve internal issues and problems will set the standard for the rest of the world. World, be prepared. The *American Spirit* in action will be a sight to behold. Prepare for a new era of thought, action and opportunity.

On these grounds, I request the unity and collaborative participation on these matters. While the issues and concerns are difficult to refute, just where the American People stand in the process has cannot be in question. Therefore, instead of remaining apathetic or gazing at each other with suspicious or doubtful prejudices, let each of us hold out to our neighbor the hearty hand of friendship, and unite to forgive and may we forget every former dissention. Let the names of Republican and Democrat, other political parties and all the offensive names of race, culture and gender be extinguished; and let none other be heard among us, than those of a good citizen, an open and resolute friend, and a virtuous supporter of the CONSTITUTION OF THE UNITED STATES OF AMERICA and THE BILL OF RIGHTS and every American's right to LIFE, LIBERTY AND THE PURSUIT OF HAPPINESS.

The Crisis Overview (1995)

Introduction

Common Sense by Thomas Paine was published in early 1776 and was a major influence on the Declaration of Independence, adopted on July 4, 1776. *The Crisis* by Thomas Paine was written in

December 1776 for motivational purposes and read to General Washington's desperate troops. The initial excitement of the Declaration had begun to fade. Paine's words revived the five thousand men under General Washington's leadership, at a time when the battle for America's independence seemed at the brink of defeat. Shortly thereafter, victories were won at Trenton and at Princeton, which were considered turning points of the American Revolutionary War. It is questionable whether America faces a crisis today. It is definitely not a crisis as the one faced by the Founders of America. It is a crisis of the *American Spirit*.

In the elections of 1992 and 1994, the majority of the electorate voted for change. Now, the electorate must continue with their daily lives and maintain their faith that their elected representatives will make the necessary changes. The changes will take time. The furious activity happening in the 104th Congress makes the appearance of effecting changes, but those activities continue to happen within the framework of *Politics As Usual*. Therefore, we must maintain a vigilant watch. Why have they not addressed necessary changes regarding campaign reform? Why do they continue the political rhetoric regarding the entitlements of Social Security and Medicare? Everyone knows these must be reformed. Who has the courage? They continue to say it can be painless, but we all know that at some point, there will be pain. Our concern should be that all delays to address the real issues will only result in much greater pains in the future.[56]

Paine's writing *The Crisis*, also updated, has meaning for today, just as I updated *Thoughts on the Present State of American Affairs*. We must ask ourselves if the right things are happening today, in order for our future to be the way we expect and want it to be. This is the question that stands before us all. If labeling it as a crisis now keeps us on our toes and averts a real crisis, then maybe our children might have cause to sing praises to us. Now, that would be change![57]

---

56 There is nothing more to say other than the pain is definitely upon the American people in 2012.

57 It is doubtful, based upon the current course and direction. Our children and progeny will only wonder why our generation failed future generations so miserably.

The Crisis (1995)

> The following has been revised, adapted and updated from the original publications in 1776 by Thomas Paine, entitled *The Crisis*.

These are times that try all people's souls. The truly apathetic, unreasonable and selfish American will, in this crisis, shrink from their duty and service to America. Those who stand now deserve the love and thanks of every man, woman and child. *Politics As Usual*, like one's dependency on drugs, is not easily overcome. While we are already pursuing various rewards for our personal and family's enrichment, we must realize our duty to God, country and the children. Our parents and grandparents fought and died in battles and deserve our blessing and respect for maintaining America's freedom. From their conflict, they rejoiced glorious triumphs. From them, we learned the lesson, that, which we obtain too cheaply, we esteem too lightly. It is often the struggle itself that truly gives everything its value. Freedom's true value is unknown until it is lost. It would be strange indeed if we honored our forbearers by allowing ourselves to be conquered from within by the tyranny of POLITICS AS USUAL. *Politics As Usual* produces nothing and infects young and old minds alike with visions of power. Only simple government, lead by authentic, dignified, duty-minded leaders is all that should exist for our children.

The status quo, with all its lobbyists, politicians, bureaucrats, excessive regulations, government appointees, government employees and apathetic electorate is a vast, blameless army which sustains the tyranny of *Politics As Usual*. By default and apathy, *We the People* have allowed *Politics As Usual* to assume the right to not only tax and spend and to mortgage our children's futures, *but it has intertwined some form of government regulation and taxes into EVERY ASPECT OF SOCIETY*. By being bound in this manner, *We the People* are as indentured servants (part-time slaves) and no agreement exists which gives any politician or bureaucrat the right to have such unlimited power over society.

It is the electorate's fallibility to overlook their personal democratic duty for the sake of convenience. Our human inclination to tolerate many abuses before making changes has allowed *Politics As Usual,* specifically career politicians and bureaucrats to remain too long, in the presence of temptation with the people's money. Adam Smith is quoted as saying,

> *"There is no art which one government sooner learns of another than that of draining money from the pockets of the people."*

America's government is a government of the people, by the people and for the people. The only unlimited power over society should belong only to God. Even God leaves us to our own choices and devices.

Whether the removal of *Politics As Usual* has come too soon or delayed too long, there is no need for argument and most of us have the simple opinion that, had it been twenty years earlier, it would have been much better.[58]

I believe, without the fear of reprisal, that the *Faithful Majority,* filled with their *American Spirit,* firmly rooted in the faith and belief in God will now declare and act to make things the way they should be. Those who have so earnestly and so repeatedly sought to make things right will now be joined by the *Faithful Majority* in such numbers, leaving no doubt to the wisdom and methods of common sense and natural reason. Neither do I have so much of a *Pollyanna* attitude, as to suppose that the status quo, deeply embedded, will relinquish their position in *Politics As Usual* willingly. Likewise the fear of change and reform will strike heavy upon those citizens who have given themselves to and become dependent upon the government programs. Many now believe that they are entitled. And the unknown consequences of accepting personal responsibility for much of society's issues and problems where government has failed will strain and test the very fabric of American society. Yet, I believe that America's diverse society will exhibit the wisdom and reason that only a free nation of over two hundred years is capable of doing. The *Faithful Majority* will make it happen and make things the way they should be.

---

58   How many times has the Author said, this should have changed twenty years
      ago, in 1995 and today it is 2012.

There is much to question and issues in which to be concerned, but no one individual should pretend to be disadvantaged and presume they are entitled to the people's money, when in reality they are capable of being a contribution to society. Immense changes have transformed much of society over the last fifty years. Outdated beliefs regarding political legislative activities, legal system abuses, education, health, welfare, social security and various other government programs have allowed for abuse. But, primarily it has been the programs themselves which have created even greater problems than those which they were originally established to resolve.

There is no place on earth that has the individual rights and freedoms as we do in America. Our situation is envied by other self-reliant and self-motivated individuals around the world, primarily for America's enterprising spirit. Yet, America has failings unparalleled by any other nation in the world. Americans have the freedom to distinguish themselves by their culture, race, creed or gender. I am confident, as I am that the *American Spirit* will prevail, that America will resolve many more of its issues and problems when all or the vast majority of Americans join in a spirit of unity and collaborative participation. Violence, AIDS, television violence, political party stagnation and alienation, burdensome regulations, deficit spending; and bureaucratic funding abuses will all continue until the time when the *Faithful Majority* stand within the eternal flame of liberty. If there must be change, let it be in my day so that my children may have the freedom to determine their own destinies and not be burdened with my cowardice.

I turn with the warm appreciation of a friend to those who have nobly stood, and are yet determined to stand the matter out; I call not upon a few but upon every American. If a private enterprise does not perform reasonable service or produce quality merchandise for the price, then an individual can express their dissatisfaction. The enterprise does not have the luxury to ignore its obligation to its customers. Why then, do government bureaucrats, paid by the people's money and servant to the people, have the right to ignore the people's voice of dissatisfaction and why do our elected representatives feed this process and allow these injustices to continue?

It is best the *Faithful Majority* and the electorate should exhibit more of their power than too little when so great an object is at stake. Let it be told to the future world that in the face of *Politics As Usual,* the majority showed their faith by their works in the spirit of unity and collaborative participation. It matters not where one lives, financial status or standing in the community. The burdens or the blessings will reach us all. Our delays will increase the suffering. Our actions will have us all rejoicing. The heart that refuses these actions now is dead; the blood of their children will curse their cowardice who shrinks back at a time when a little might have saved the whole and made them happy. I love anyone that can smile in trouble that can gather strength from chaos and become stronger and more confident by their persistence. Little minds will shrink from these matters. They who pursue with all their heart the truths, values and principles of America's heritage are the true American heroes in who we have searched for or sought after.

My own line of reasoning is to myself as straight and clear as a laser. I do not propose abolishment of our American government. I propose removing the immense burden of billions of dollars of government waste and excessive regulations, which robs productive individuals and American enterprise of billions of dollars of capital. This capital in the hands of productive individuals and enterprise will unleash a tidal wave of American progress never before paralleled in American history.

Nor am I without compassion for those truly in need of the people's care. I propose serious review of the regulations concerning government bureaucracies, defense and welfare, but more importantly Social Security and Medicare. The vast entanglements on the variety of issues of States rights and Federal Government mandates and government's *Great Society* programs has transferred society's sense of caring and compassion from the family and community by displacing it to a compassionless and special interest driven government. This has been a choice of convenience for the electorate. At the same time, the electorate had a misguided *Utopian* expectation that government would be the caretaker for all the disadvantaged. No one ever expected that the bureaucracies would actually produce so many more disadvantaged. Now we know this false-sense of security that society has transferred to government cannot long endure.

Alan W. Goldsberry

Americans work and produce like never before. Wages, income and earnings are beyond any conventional wisdom of twenty-five years ago and yet, statistics are being presented saying household incomes have declined. At the same time; statistics also present that a greater percentage of households have incomes of $50,000 or more compared to ten years ago. Who is right? What makes a difference is whether or not an individual has the opportunity to pursue their own desires of happiness with the least amount of regulations and the merry-go-round of *Politics As Usual*, which benefits a few and burdens the majority.

All the various, combined levels of government receive trillions of dollars to do the work the electorate has passed on to its various elected representatives. Those representatives have produced such voluminous legislation that armies of professionals are necessary to dot the i's and cross the t's. The average American must hire these legions of professionals in order to reduce the risk of reprisal from a government agency or bureaucrat. Necessary government programs were enacted by compassionate politicians and managed by duty-minded individuals as the answer to society's prayers during times in American history, when large portions of society needed a helping hand. And rightly so, equality of opportunity has been deservedly given to all Americans. Now these programs are maintained by *Politics As Usual* and career bureaucrats, as their personal fiefdoms.

Our progeny will have history for a clear view of that which has transpired and developed during these times. We do not have that advantage of reviewing what we must do before it is done; and yet we must act. We must take the risks. Our progeny will both admire and hold in reverence the legacy we create for them, as we do with America's Founding Fathers. Or, our progeny will admonish us and hold us in disdain for our lack of courage, apathy and denial of our personal responsibility in the matters at hand. No matter the outcome, I believe they will admire our convictions and actions. Our travesty will be our knowing and not acting. This is what our progeny will not understand.

There are situations which cannot be overdone by any amount of written or verbal communication, and this is one. There are persons who do not see the full extent of the issues and the problems which threaten them. They continue to believe in *Politics*

110

As Usual, because they think it is stronger and mightier. Those who believe this have simply lost their personal sense of power, self-respect, and that they personally can be important and make a difference. It is madness to believe that doing the same thing over and over, with more money and people will produce a different result. It might appear good and seem to make the most sense, but it is a feeble and costly attempt of making a good show, instead of dealing with real issues and making things the way they should be.

The role of government and the role of society will forever be discussed and debated. This is the true wisdom of our Founding Fathers - a form of government that allows for an ongoing process of growth and development of a nation and its society. Let no one question America's testament to freedom and an individual's rights to life, liberty and the pursuit of happiness. The Power of the electorate decides this matter. The majority rules. The question at hand is who will become the majority of the people and what will the majority of the people do? By perseverance and fortitude, we have the prospect of a glorious triumph for all Americans; by apathy and submission, a sad choice of a variety of *evils*. Let the *Faithful Majority* stand and be the power that makes it the way it should be.

PART FOUR
And So...It Continues(1995)

These are times that try men's souls.

~ Thomas Paine ~

A Convergence of Choices (1995)

America, once again, has arrived at an unprecedented *convergence of choices*. The choices available to an individual today extend across a wide range of beliefs and lifestyles. Two hundred years of free enterprise, motivated individuals, a tolerant society, a simple, effective government structure and peaceful changes in political power have brought forth unexpected opportunities and unrealized expectations. These choices, motivated and realized for the purposes of profit, power, desired lifestyles and humane concerns will not be relinquished by free individuals. Likewise, the issues, problems and challenges facing society and government will not be easily resolved, nor will the power held by politicians and bureaucrats be easily replaced in the *good hands* of society. They will say they fear that society will once again limit human rights. I say they fear the losses of their personal power structures they have built into individual fiefdoms. Politicians and bureaucrats feel they have the *right* to hold power over the disadvantaged and to maintain the ever-suggestive threat of a power over the advantaged.

Change is inevitable and the choice of the changes must eventually reside with each responsible individual. The broad spectrum of choices available today continues to expand, but at a rate controlled by a multitude of legislative actions and bureaucratic regulations. America's social issues and problems likewise are being hampered by bureaucratic regulatory attempts to make everyone equal. The *"disadvantaged"* dependent upon the programs have little, if any choice, and individuals from society wanting to assist to make a difference have to abide by so many other regulations their choices are likewise limited in what can be accomplished. Broad-brush government programs and tax increases *on the rich* is an attempt to re-distribute wealth by politicians to look good to the *have-nots* and prey upon the compassions of the electorate. This has never worked and its impact would be minimal, given a four trillion dollar debt and a two hundred to three hundred billion dollar annual deficit.[59] All actions by politicians are for the sake of *Politics As Usual* and for re-election. Their promises of government aid and lower taxes are a con-job. The cowardice of the politicians, power-hungry bureaucrats and apathetic electorate are not designed by a single tyrant. No tyrant who ever lived could have dreamed of having so many people with all the appearances of working at odds with one another, when in reality are working beautifully together to restrain and limit the individual. Maybe this is why so many *Socialist* nations are now grasping the value of democracy. It has the perceptions of liberty, yet in reality, provides benefits beyond any such experiences of previous socialist or communist leaders.

At this point of convergence in American history, the choices now by the electorate will be the action to produce a quantum leap in America or continue the slow, downward spiral of ever-imposing limitations on future choices.[60] If personal incomes and

---

59   Those were the Good Ole Days, right? Only the obvious is abundantly clear. In less than twenty years, these issues are now triple in scope. You've got to think that over this past twenty years there have been leaders who desired to make the right changes and I can only consider how their soul laments for not being one who made the right things happen. And, then, there are those elected politicians who had and still do not have any desires to do what's right for America. They only live for their self-centered ambitions.

60   In the midst of change, there are various points of bifurcation. These points of bifurcation are a splitting or branching off into two separate parts. In this example of a "slow, downward spiral" – that is the way it looks shortly after the point of bifurcation. As time progresses and without another point of bifurcation to alter the downward spiral, the spiraling process accelerates like a penny being place in one of those funnels used in establishments to raise money for a meaningful cause. The penny starts out slowly circling the top of the funnel and then it quickly accelerates, spinning faster and faster around the funnel until it drops into the container below. I assert that tripling of the national debt and deficit in less than twenty years demonstrates the reality of

standards of living have been declining over the past two decades, where is the common sense to correlate the growth of big government with declining personal incomes?

These are times that try all people's souls. America is a strong, diverse, multi-cultural nation fragmented by the past forty years of debates and struggles for individual rights and equality of opportunity. Many have fought for the dream of realizing the promises of the United States Constitution to its fullest potential. The legislative process and the legal system have been the battlefield of choice. The time for these battles to cease is now. To continue this process works against the freedoms and choices that has been achieved. As in 1776, the *voice of reason* and common sense, once again, screams loudly in our ears here and now in 1995. The path of unity and collaborative participation will allow our individual choices and freedoms to expand and opportunities that appear over the horizon will be realized and will be available to all Americans and our progeny.

There are some who think that since we are all created equal, then it is government's role to keep all of humanity equal. Never in the history of the world has the promise of equalized utopia been realized. America has achieved her greatness by the grace of God, the courage of America's Founders and the freedom of the *American Spirit* to pursue the potential for success. The freedom to choose by our forbearers has brought America to this point in history. They continually chose to reign in the size of federal government. If they had chosen the ways of big government and maintained it in an earlier period in history, then we would not be faced with the questions placed before America today. We would be **without** these challenging questions, our abundant freedoms and variety of choices that exist today.

The questions, concerns and issues of the individual and the roles of society and government rests, once again, at the touchstone of humanity [touchstone – any test or criterion for determining genuineness or value]. **We, the People** have tolerated the powerful influences of business, while knowing of their designs

---

how close America is to dropping off into the abyss below. It is time for a meaningful point of bifurcation that creates a quantum leap upward and forward.

for profit and market expansion and their actions have always continued to expand individual choices and individual wealth. While free enterprise has increased individual choices, the burdens and intrusions of government have worked to limit choices in the name of compassion and human rights. In reality it has been the power struggle between business and *Politics As Usual*. As Paine wrote,

> *Society is produced by our wants, and government by our wickedness; the former promotes our happiness positively by uniting our affections, the latter negatively by restraining our vices. The one encourages intercourse, the other creates distinctions. The first is a patron, the last a punisher.*61

Doors of vast opportunities have continued to open – satisfying society's wants and filling the needs of a diverse, multi-cultural society. At the same time, the unrealized expectations in regards to social issues, problems and challenges have been uncovered and have been revealed continually by the special interests and biased media. Government, in its wickedness, has actually increased the number of *"disadvantaged"* in order to have more power (by making extreme distinctions thus defaulting to become in reality, the punisher).62

In society's general pursuit of individual ambitions, compassion has not been lost, simply displaced through government's incessant intervention into our private lives. Politician's expressions of compassion and caring, so society could continue its ambitious pursuits; in time reveal only their personal self-interests and ambitions. It is just the nature of the allure of power given to those of weak character and personal values. Americans are not without compassion, for they step forward time and again, without question, in times of disasters and local community needs. Yet,

---

61   The example of the confluence of the Ohio and Mississippi rivers, along with the concept of Both/And thinking encourage discourse and, as Paine refers, intercourse – all with the intention to create a new alternative – something greater than the two individual rivers.

62   Government programs such as welfare, social security, Medicare and now Obamacare prove just how government left unchecked will continually create such programs that assimilate the many, like the Borg in Star Trek.

generally, society has depended upon government to resolve issues perceived by society as broad, major social issues. It is time for it to be realized that these social issues are not a mass of people all needing the same care and treatment. These broad social issues are comprised of many distinct individuals, who have been lumped together and restricted to similar benefits. Their freedom of choice has been severely limited, and they have been robbed of their unalienable rights to life, liberty and the pursuit of happiness. Like society, they have depended too long on government. Government has become a compassionless caretaker and government's attempts have generally failed, given the changes of the times. In this process, the distinction between society and government has become, as Thomas Paine wrote, *so confounded.*

American's pursuits of the choices of happiness, prosperity and opportunities have resulted in the majority of Americans lounging in the luxury of liberty for too long. The majority of Americans have not had to risk death for their freedom. Nor have the majority of Americans truly entered into a discourse of the truths, principles and values that the Founding Fathers understood, debated and risked their lives for. As Thomas Paine wrote, *"What we obtain too cheap, we esteem too lightly."*

My purpose for writing *Common Sense Revisited* and bringing together the writings of America's Founders and other authors was to stimulate such a discourse, so that many more Americans would grow to understand and take on the wisdom of America's Founders and their abilities to think through situations that required very different thinking to create new alternatives. The majority of Americans can no longer ignore the call of duty to sustain the eternal flame of liberty.

Thread of Concern (1995)

A thread of concern, discontent and insecurity weaves throughout America. It is not a pipeline as in times of war or a national depression. It is a mere thread, which begins in the home, winding its way through the neighborhoods, into the schools, throughout the community, to the state capitals and makes its way into Washington, D.C. When it reaches Washington, D.C., its frayed end is quickly snipped and re-spun to fit the needs for weaving the selfish designs of the special interests.

Is America in a crisis? No other superpower threatens our freedom. There are no soldiers of the government to break down our doors. No financial crisis wreaks havoc through every community in the nation.[63] The widespread protests and unrest of the 1960's achieved much and have since matured. The majority of our lives are spent at work, with family and participation in various parts of the community. We work hard. We play and enjoy a vast variety of interests. We enjoy independence and we are willing to make many allowances and suffer many injustices to maintain the lifestyles we enjoy. Yet, the thread exists.

Will this thread ever become a national or worldwide crisis?[64] There are various possibilities for our future if a direction is not determined and taken. The obvious choice is the continued expansion of free-enterprise and individual choices. Yet, many fiefdoms of power have been created throughout government. Should we make this a crisis before a real crisis appears? The only reason might be to call forth the determination of the *Faithful Majority* and the leadership style that has been admired by Americans for two hundred and twenty years. The style of leadership that steps up in times of crisis, maintains dignity, is accountable, tells the truth and makes the tough decisions. Their leadership style, courage and actions inspire people to join together in a sense of unity and cooperation – leaders like George Washington, Thomas Jefferson, Abraham Lincoln, Franklin Roosevelt...

---

63 Remember this was written in 1995. Since that time, there has been 9/11 and the largest financial crisis since the Great Depression. The Author now asserts that if the Faithful Majority wait much longer to express their concerns, discontent and insecurity – the Fiscal Cliff receiving so much press could very well become our reality.

64 This should be the wake-up call we all hear. The changes now are an overhaul of the entitlement programs and the extreme abuses of the political system by the elected politicians and now it is being reported even the Federal employees are gaming the system for their personal benefit. Everything from theft and fraud to not filing their personal income tax. It is time for a change. Not more blustering oration of blame and ridicule. Real, substantial, significant and sustainable change is preferred now, not later.

Times of crisis have brought forth true leadership where it least likely resided. However leadership over the past several decades has been scattered and fragmented throughout America. In perspective, we must remember America was not a great, developed nation in 1776. The Founding Fathers represented a few small communities. Yet even as a young start-up nation, the Founders and succeeding leaders faced excessive national debts, social issues and unrest, a civil war, riots and foreign matters of concern. Today, wise leaders with the values and principles of America's Founders exist throughout every community and industry of America. In his book, *Global Paradox,* John Naisbitt describes global paradox as: *The bigger the world economy, the more powerful its smallest players.* Has that not always been the case throughout world history? An individual or small group of individuals start a movement that appeals to the Faithful Majority. That is what makes the difference. A small group without the Faithful Majority cannot be sustainable and will remain labeled as extremist. Except now nations and businesses are *so big* and the individual appears *so small,* yet technologies are always developed to level the playing field for individuals to become leaders with power to secure or maintain their inalienable rights. Today we have computers and telecommunications linking us to the world through a variety of computer networks. These modern day *power tools* give an individual as much computing power on their desk, as most major corporations had twenty years ago.[65]

This *truly American style of leadership* also exists within the ranks of the elected leaders in politics today, yet they have been left to their own devices and in the temptation of the peoples' money for too long. In the process, they have become stewards for their political party, the status quo, the special interests and their own self interests – as opposed to their position and duty of being representatives for the people and for the good of America. They work hard, yet the duty they perform as representatives for their constituents are questionable, as it well should be. They should be concerned for their jobs for every day that passes without

---

65 While the internet was just in its infancy, no one imagined what it would become in less than twenty years. And, now mobile has burst on the scene. We can only imagine the possibilities.

meaningful changes being made. It is seen more for the *politics it really is*. The purpose of their actions seems to always be with the designs of re-election. Already the positioning for the 1996 elections has begun. What will Congress accomplish for the rest of 1995 and most of 1996? What do these politicians, who are now positioning for 1996, plan to make happen now? Not two or four years from now.[66]

If they do have a plan and have America's interests as their primary concern, why do they bicker over the same issues time and time again? Why does this gridlock remain? Why do they not pass true campaign reform before the 1996 elections? Why do they set such unworthy examples of leadership for our children when they are running for political office? The things they say about one another are nothing better than children on a playground. This is a lesson for children to learn. As adults, especially political leaders, they should set the example – be a model. Yet, they parade around as little children, not as mature adults. They do not deserve to be called leaders.[67] Where is their dignity? Why do they not write their own speeches and stand before their constituents honestly? Why does ineffective party partisanship continue to take precedence over solutions and genuine actions? If they were genuinely working for the majority, why the need for such volumes of legislation? Why the continued pork barrel and earmarks for votes. If the

---

66   The Author only had conjecture in 1995. Now, it is history and, for those willing to dive deep to learn and know the truth can find the actual records of the information that cannot be denied, no matter how many times some politician changes their message, based upon the latest poll. Relative to the housing crisis, written, audio and video records exist to show what the politicians were saying in 2007 and how in 2009, they denied ever saying the things said in 2007 or earlier. How can the Faithful Majority continue to allow such liars to hold such positions of power? The truth is those liars either think they are always telling the truth or they think the Faithful Majority is just a barrel of monkeys.

67   The real shame in the behavior of these immature politicians is how they attack others and exclaim how others should be better role models for our children. Yet, in an instant, if a TV camera is turned their way, they will offer up some degrading remark about their opponent – and, believe what they do stands above reproach. To these politicians, beware. You are marked for who you are and re-election will be a distant memory for you, soon.

legislation is right and good for America, why the use of graft and extortion to gain one more vote? Such a monster has been created in the process of government, that elected leaders have removed themselves from the true American values and principles. It is time for them to once again, "Stand with and for All Americans."

The genius and power of the design of American government is its three distinct branches of government, which is designed to limit the possibility of tyranny. What the Founders never conceived was that the elected leaders would cower from their responsibility as elected representatives. The politicians, for reasons of selfishness, now in reality create and maintain such dissention among the three branches, as opposed to respecting, deliberating and reaching a consensus in the best interests of all Americans. In this cowardice process, bureaucracy has become a fourth branch of government, out of control and operating as if it is beyond the scope of the Constitution. Only the most courageous of leaders need apply for the future leadership of America.

Thomas Paine stated it quite well when he wrote:

> *"The summer soldier and the sunshine patriot will, in this crisis, shrink from the service of their country;[68] but he that stands it now, deserves the love and thanks of man and woman. Tyranny, like hell, is not easily conquered; yet we have this consolation with us, that the harder the conflict, the more glorious the triumph. What we obtain too cheap, we esteem too lightly; it is dearness only that gives everything its value. Heaven knows how to put a proper price upon its goods; and it would be strange indeed if so celestial an article as FREEDOM should not be highly rated."*

---

68   Has the American public not witnessed such an outcome – the absolute stalemate between the parties? Neither willing to step forward as authentic leaders for they fear the retribution of their political bullies as opposed to doing what's right for America. The so called leaders of each political party is nothing more than a bully. They cannot be called leaders. Maybe it's time for an authentic leader like Benjamin Franklin to step forward with a call to prayer, unity and collaborative participation.

The stewards residing in the leadership of American politics have recently felt the sting of the power of the electorate (the real power in America). Yet, the old habits of the status quo will not change until they see the new status quo of the *Faithful Majority*. It is time for the majority of Americans to join together and perform their duty as the electorate. Until that time, *Politics As Usual* will be maintained. It is time for all Americans to act with the *American Spirit* that has made America great.

Our true *American Spirit* has lain dormant within the challenges facing America. The *American Spirit* does not reside within the flag-waving of party politics. It resides within the hearts and souls of every American and the everyday ordinary, authentic actions of the *Faithful Majority*. Although America has been separated and fragmented over the last few decades, this process has actually strengthened many Americans with the knowledge and wisdom of leadership, the likes of which birthed America. The words of wisdom from the Founders now speak clearly and their accomplishments ring loudly. Political leaders today speak and write the same words from only hollow shells, with the appearances of courage and they are without accomplishment. While the issues of society and government are vast and difficult, no other nation's peoples have neither the willingness nor the capacity to face and deal with these complex and difficult issues. The *Faithful Majority* stand ready. Elected leaders have only to set aside their selfish designs of *Politics As Usual* and request the resources of the *Faithful Majority*. (Do not ask for financial contributions. Ask for those resources that make things happen). Elected politicians need to take decisive action. If it is right for America, they will be re-elected. Why not measure their accomplishments as any executive officer of a private or public company? It appears the politicians make laws that protect them from such measurements.

America's system of government works. We have only to work the system, with the wisdom, dignity and justice, in which it was intended – not the way *We, the People* have allowed the stewards of government to do. Some will recite the polls that say Americans talk a good game, but they are not willing to put forth the efforts necessary. These are words of immature politicians who think the Faithful Major is only a myth. For example; several polls have asked Americans if they want lower taxes. They say, "Yes." When asked if they will personally sacrifice, the answer is "No." Other polls have asked if certain government programs should be done away with, such as Welfare. The answer is "Yes." When asked if Americans will pick up the slack, the answer is "No." While these dichotomies may exist in sterile polls, the *American Spirit* in action can neither be explained nor legislated. It has only the results of its actions in history to point. We the common folks in America are ready to "GET THE JOB DONE!" When will authentic leaders emerge who have the courage to ask for the sacrifices that must be made? Few people today have any understanding of the sacrifices colonists made for America to achieve its independence. One can hear the empty words spoken of those who have died in wars to maintain our freedom – yet, few truly appreciate just how close America came to not becoming this great nation. With minimal study and research, anyone can discover that similar political attitudes and selfishness almost caused the War for Independence to fail. It came down to a few authentic leaders. If not for the likes of George Washington and Robert Morris, it is very likely we would all be saying "cheerio" and that would not be a request for a favorite breakfast cereal. And, one cannot deny the providence of God, without which this nation cannot not survive, much less thrive.

The tasks that lie before America will be done. The outcomes will be accomplished for the betterment of America. *We, the People* (this includes the political leaders) will perform our duty and bring forth the true promises of the Declaration of Independence and The Constitution of the United States.[69]

The process of America's development has not been consistent, nor could it have been planned. It has been the enviable *American Spirit*, the melting pot of the world's people, who have had the individual freedom of choice to pursue their personal, family and community dreams. By our wise and common-sense actions now, we acknowledge and demonstrate our thanks to the Founding

---

[69] Yes, the Author remains hopeful and faithful that the right leaders will emerge and this great nation will once again thrive in ways the world will envy and emulate. It only takes a few courageous leaders because most politicians are weak and without the ability to make something happen.

Fathers for creating a beginning, which has been continually developed by wise and courageous leaders during the past two hundred years. Common sense, personal dignity, the providence of God and duty to the people is the model for us all to aspire to achieve.

As the next chapter of America unfolds, the majority of Americans are waking up to the real values of freedom. Our cultural differences have always been our strength for America. Now, these cultural differences, unified and cooperating within the context of equality of opportunities must break apart old habits, biases and prejudices, unprecedented by any conventional wisdom.[70]

We should pray we will repeat the best parts of history. Those parts filled with the wisdom and insight into the soul of humanity. Things have changed – change has always resulted for the good – and the Faithful Majority needs to come to an agreement that government now must change.

And so...it continues. *We, the People* continue America's forward progress.

---

70 Much in this vain of thought and equality have been achieved. My sons [and our future daughters-in-law] do not live with the ugly, out-dated prejudices my generation grew up with and had to endure. The racial and countless prejudices that have kept us divided have become like the confluence of the Ohio and Mississippi rivers. We have only to move along-side one another to realize the dreams of many. It has been interesting observing the maturing of my sons who are without the prejudices I experienced at their age. They are an example of how nature works when people are allowed to self-govern with common sense, reason and basic human rights. There is no question that great things are at hand and to come in the future and neither should we forget the chaos and segregation of America's past.

Alan W. Goldsberry

Stay the Course (1995)

Man must cease attributing his problems to his environment and learn again to exercise his free will - his personal responsibility in the realm of faith and morals.

~ Albert D. Switzer ~

Change is inevitable. In a progressive country change is constant.

~ Benjamin Disraeli ~

Change has begun. Will it stay on course? Will elected leaders be the representatives they have been elected to be – and lead the way to reducing the federal deficit, reducing the size and intrusiveness of government in the process and renewing the *American Spirit?*[71]

An infinite power exists within humanity beyond any national power or political party ever created in the world – a power beyond control or description in the present moment. The Author believes this power to be a gift from God. This indescribable power reveals itself in historical accounts by those defining moments, when an unlikely leader emerges and individuals are inspired and mobilized into action. The subsequent tangible outcomes of their actions then lay vulnerable for posterity's historic review – either with acclaim or consternation.

The Founding Fathers and all colonists stand as a testament to this power. Their actions and beliefs provided the guiding words of the United States Constitution. *We, the People of the United States of America,...* We can hold judgment upon their prejudices until we turn blue, but we were not there in that time. We are here now and the question at hand – what will you do, now? Stand in judgment or jump into the reality of today and seek to make a

---

71   Reminder this was originally written in 1995. The original writing has been left to demonstrate the results of the past twenty years – and to provide some understanding that this is the way America's political system works. The Author remains hopeful and faithful – and, he is re-introducing this book in the hopes it will awaken others to the need for action, now.

difference instead of speak of things that are long gone and, in truth, have been or are being resolved in ways, no one can fathom or understand until history reviews and reveals the truth.

We, the People, (that's us folks) stand, as our forbearers, at the threshold of a new era. We stand knowing we have a duty to serve to sustain America's incredible journey. It is our time and America's destiny calls to us all. Although actions recently, either by design or default seem to make the statement – *They, the People.* Apathy and blame have been the choice of participation because the issues and problems seem vast and unsolvable. Some of the best minds in America have addressed these issues. They have not failed; they have not received the support of all Americans. So, elected leaders today fear further attempts because they must have the support of the people. They do not wish to fail.[72]

There is no single tyrant or political faction that we all can easily point to as the creator of the problems. The political parties and other special interests continually blame one another, but that is for self-serving purposes to achieve more power, but power over what if they continue to fail? Political Party Leadership, the status quo and the special interests believe *"The Power"* resides with them. This is an illusionary power. They easily forget the kindergarten lesson; when one points the finger, three fingers point back to them.[73]

The elections of November 1994 delivered a message like that of an earthquake. An earthquake can be a fast, ruthless reminder that humanity cannot fool around with Mother Nature. The political parties, status quo and special interests should also realize they cannot fool around with America's electorate or the *Faithful Majority.*[74]

---

72 And, fail they have at managing the Federal Deficit and massive debt. Many are trying to correct the wrongs, but lack the leadership skills to make it happen.

73 Sounds like a broken record on this one. The blame game has been vaulted to Olympic records over the past three years.

74 Sadly, and it seems I've used that word too often; the politicians have taken advantage of the Faithful Majority. While many voices of reason and common sense have attempted to awaken the Faithful Majority, the opposing

For those who believe the power resides in *Politics As Usual* and the political rhetoric of promises, commitments and contracts, continually made to the American electorate, will once again suffice and appease the electorate, do not realize the electorate already sees the fabric of the promises as loosely weaved and contracts already appeared frayed and tattered. Just like a flag secured to a pole and left exposed to the harsh elements of the weather for too long. Changing winds can be the harshest. The old flag should be brought down and placed on display and acknowledged as the symbol of its accomplishments to the nation before it is tattered beyond recognition. To allow a flag to wither away is like allowing our memories to forget the challenges and sacrifices made by so many. Let the Faithful Majority be raised upon the pole like a new flag, symbolizing the renewal of the *American Spirit*. This should be quickly raised and flown in joyous celebration of American pride at its best with the memories of those who sacrificed themselves and the recognition of our call to duty.

The real power, the electorate of America, has spoken. Ongoing, new legislation and ever expanding bureaucracies, which may have good appearances, are in reality smothering. A looming shadow of doubt can be observed on the faces of America's elected leaders. They know change is inevitable, yet they resist because of their fears of the unknown and their misplaced representation to the status quo and special interests. Current political leadership has a choice. They can be a part of the inevitable changes or not. The American electorate has made their choice and it is clear, *Politics As Usual* will not be allowed to continue.[75]

---

side has sought to use the power of the media to discredit those as extremists. The abuse in the power of the media has also fallen into the hands of ignorant mouthpieces who read tele-prompters to relay what they want the public to believe are their individual thoughts and opinions. Thank God for the Internet and the availability of information and discourse beyond the media pundits. This is actually the way it was during the early days of the American Revolution. There were thousands of printing machines producing Broadsides and Pamphlets, composed of multiple thoughts and opinions. Very much like the Internet, today.

75   Are we truly ready for the right things to happen in order to change the obvious course of destruction that awaits us all? Obviously, time will tell – and, the only way to be assured of what is to come is to begin to think and

The *Faithful Majority* now must leave no doubts of the way things should be and remember prior accomplishments throughout America's heritage. America's Founders, in spite of the odds, uncertainties and the unknown they faced, their actions exemplified one of Goethe's couplets: *"Whatever you can do, or dream you can, begin it. Boldness has genius, power, and magic in it."*

The Path Already Exists (1995)

The Founders risked their lives and gave their lives to achieve the dream of freedom and liberty. In the process of achieving their dream, divine intervention happened. For the first time in the history of the world, the truths, principles and values which are the absolute birthright of every human became the founding truths, principles and values of a system of government. While the Founders lived during a period of time that limited human rights for some people existing in America, it cannot be denied the broad framework they secured in the Constitution allowed for the realization of inalienable rights for all Americans to eventually become reality.

Who can deny that the opening words of the Constitution, **We, the People** has not been a guiding light for Americans to achieve the goal of equal rights for all Americans. If this were not so, why did so many die, of all races and cultures, in the American civil war? Why did so many, of all races and cultures again, stand up during the civil rights movement? Those who gave their lives still touch our hearts and souls because we knew them, either by television, newspaper or in person.

America, from experiment to status of greatest nation, has endured ongoing intervention of human self-interests. There have been many trials and tribulations, chaos, mood swings, good times, bad times and the perpetual pendulum swings from left to right of political thought. No matter the situation, circumstance or the unknown enormity of the task at hand, the American people have always stood up to the test, endured and overcome. In this process, America and its peoples have gained new strengths, discovered

act in ways that are more likely to bring your hopes and dreams into reality.

new, abundant resources, realized new growth opportunities in the midst of chaos and received insightful wisdom to sustain the *American Dream* for future generations.

It is time once again for America's leaders to lead in a determined direction of greatness. Inspire all Americans to be the best they can be. It is not the time for elected leaders to hide-away in Washington behind all the legislative process and speak of empty promises for less legislation and regulations, while in fact they are creating more. It is time for elected leaders to lead and take the heat of their inaction or get out of the kitchen so someone who will fulfill the duty of being a representative of the people can emerge. It is not the time for reform by introducing more or better procedures. It is time for revolution of the *American Spirit.* Risks are certain and the rewards are unknown. America has stood the test before and has come forth greater each time. Why would true leaders hesitate at such a moment in history?[76]

The design of American government and its cornerstone, The Constitution of the United States and Bill of Rights are not in question. What remains in question are the decades of building a mountain of laws and regulations on top of the original truths of the Constitution. Many of these laws and regulations were necessary to achieve equal opportunity for all Americans and secure America's position of greatest nation in the world. Let the laws that make sense stand. Remove the intrusive and binding bureaucracies on the *American Spirit* and remove the opportunities of special interest having direct and financial influence on the legislative process. Every American has witnessed the chaos, confusion, inefficient and often times ineffective bureaucratic processes of government. All Americans are frustrated, including those working within the bureaucratic systems. We have all become imprisoned by the regulations and the systems. Some may feel this is the best security for the people, but where is the equality or

---

76   This question truly grabs at the heart of the matter for those in political office. How can they think what they do makes a difference? How can they go to sleep at night or take off on a junket of enjoyment disguised as "for the people?" Why do they hesitate? Is it out of fear of the future or the unknown? If so, they should resign today and make room for someone who can endure these challenging times.

justice in this? It is time for all Americans to seek ways to cooperate and contribute to the process of removing this mountain of waste. The touchstone for all Americans is the preamble of The Constitution.

We, the People of the United States, in Order to form a more perfect Union, establish Justice, insure domestic Tranquility, provide for the common defense, promote the general Welfare, and secure the Blessings of Liberty to ourselves and our Posterity, do ordain and establish this Constitution for the United States of America.

The majority of Americans today know that their personal sense of security is threatened. Not the security of strong armed forces, but the security which dwells only within each individual. Government's bureaucratic systems have become a false-security of first and last resort to millions of people, robbing those individuals of their self-esteem and personal drive to be self-reliant. Elected leaders during the past several decades have chosen, by their compassion and desires of personal power, to wrap more and more Americans into this false-security blanket.[77]

The majority of Americans have now voted and delivered the message that this false-security is not the right of government. Individuals must be allowed their personal freedoms to take risks, strive and struggle to achieve personal success. That is what makes Americans the best they can be.[78]

The Republican Majority put forth their **Contract with America,** saying they will lower taxes, decrease the size of

---

77 Current political leadership has taken these entitlements to new heights with no end in sight if the current leadership remains in power.

78 A saying goes that when chaos and crisis rule for a private or public company, it is viewed as an opportunity to become more efficient and effective for future growth. When chaos and crisis rule for government it is an opportunity to expand private political agendas, grow the size of government and draw more people into reliance upon government to care for them. Recent events from 2009 to 2012 stand as an absolute testament to both of these scenarios. Business has gotten more efficient while government has grown in scope and size that boggles the mind of the Faithful Majority.

Government and reform Congress. This is a simple beginning to the process of change. Yet, this will not happen unless Democratic leaders choose to cooperate and the *Faithful Majority* maintain their electoral responsibility and assume greater responsibilities for society's needs. The mountain of issues America faces has been built over the last fifty years.[79] The mountain will not be removed in a year or two, but the electorate will know if change is moving in the right direction.

The changes required will happen only if the *Faithful Majority* exercises their rights as Americans. Then the majority of political leaders in all political parties will lead by setting the example of true cooperation. Elected leaders will deliberate and arrive at consensus, which acknowledges all Americans as opposed to any political party. Those individual elected leaders who stand with the *Faithful Majority* and separate themselves from the political rhetoric, the party politics, blaming and mud-slinging will receive the admiration and respect of America's children, just as we admire and respect America's Founders. History will record how America's elected leaders acted with courage, endured the wrath of the status quo and special interests and took the necessary bold actions on an agenda which addressed the real core issues of a government too large, too complicated and entirely too intrusive and burdensome on the average American.[80]

---

79 It is now seventy years. How many businesses and non-profit organizations do you know who still do things based upon practices, processes and procedures created seventy years ago? Let's do a quick review – horse and buggy and no telephone. How long would a business last in global competition trying to do things the old way? If you believe I'm getting absurd, you're right. Because it's absurd for today's politicians to resist making sweeping changes because the world has changed. Time and again, industry leading companies who refused to embrace change quickly died. A most recent example is Kodak. They had the digital camera technology, but didn't make the necessary changes as the competition took advantage of their lack of action.

80 We're not there yet, and getting closer. The timeline for the American Revolution took thirty-four years, from 1754 (the French and Indian War) to 1788 (ratification of the U.S. Constitution). It really becomes a question of when, not if.

The task at hand is to absolutely reduce the size of federal government, including all state, county and municipal governments.[81] This course requires absolute support from the majority of Americans. The message of personal responsibility and self-reliance must grasp the leaders of each and every community. These leaders must get in touch and realize that millions of Americans already care for their community and have been doing so for over two hundred years. Inspired and motivated citizens to unify and cooperate will do more to resolve the social and economic issues, problems and challenges than any new law, government agency or bureaucrat could ever dream of doing. As more Americans renew themselves into the *Faithful Majority* by acknowledging their personal responsibility in these matters and join those who have already been in action, the *American Dream* will be assured for all Americans and future Americans. The world will benefit as witnessed by the spread of capitalism and democracy in the last decade around the world.

The issues facing America will only be resolved by saying boldly and loudly, *"This is the way things should be"*; and facing the challenges thereof. Elected officials are forewarned to remain bold and courageous and stay the course. The elections of 1994 brought forth sweeping changes, but nothing like the changes that will happen in future elections if hesitancy and more political rhetoric is the rule regarding the matters at hand.

---

81 The economic crisis of 2008 is going a long way in reducing the size and scope of government at the state, county and municipal levels because, by law, they must balance their budgets to tax revenue. This is not so for the Federal government. When will this change?

PART FIVE
America's Ongoing Process of Improvement (1995)

"Democracy assumes that anybody from any quarter can speak, and speak truth, because his mind is not cut off from the truth. All he has to do is clear out his passions and then speak." ~ Joseph Campbell ~

Introduction

America's process of ongoing improvement has always left the nation stronger and better than it was before, as you will discover from these selected writings and speeches from American Founders and early American leaders. The issues of high taxes, large government and congressional abuses have occurred earlier in America's history. The issues have always been acknowledged by bold leaders. These leaders have taken the necessary actions and inspired others to join in creating solutions for the greatest benefit and for the greatest numbers. Natural reason and common sense permeate from these selected writings and speeches. In spite of all the historical commentaries, opinions and attempts to rewrite history, the fact remains, America is the greatest nation ever conceived and it's achievement in the history of the world cannot be denied.

The reader is encouraged to seek out books and materials of the writings and speeches of authentic, proven American leaders. These writings and the actions of these bold leaders shaped the *American Spirit*. The reader will be inspired and enlightened as they begin to realize the truths, principles and values recited in these following passages are just as applicable today for the political situations at hand and useful in one's personal process of improvement.

As I began my reading and study of America's Founders, I was inspired by their knowledge, wisdom to pursue disruptive alternatives, and courage to put to action and die for their beliefs. Through my personal struggles in the process of achieving personal successes in my life, I continually gained more and more respect for the Founder's bold actions, and gained a full appreciation of my personal responsibilities and duties to myself, family, community, God and country.

Learning history as a child, even though masked in myths and dates of occurrences, it provided a sense of pride and a common ideal in which to relate with other Americans. As an adult working to build a business in the midst of a seemingly ongoing conflict with the *conventional wisdom*** challenges everything of my personal ability to discern and reason the direction I have chosen will produce fruit and succeed.

In my review and process of re-learning some of American history as an adult, I began to recognize similarities in my reasoning and the reasoning of the individuals who made themselves accountable for the success or failure of creating a nation that was fundamentally based on natural reason and common sense. Joseph Campbell is quoted in the *Power of Myth*:

> *"All men are capable of reason. That is the fundamental principle of democracy. Because everybody's mind is capable of true knowledge, you don't have to have a special authority, or a special revelation telling you that this is the way things should be."*

I am thankful to God and America's Founders, whose bold courage provided the opportunities I have today as an American. I bless their words of wisdom, which have been preserved and exist as living documents of testimony to the Founders' wisdom and courage. They reveal the truths, principles and values of individual rights and freedoms. I acknowledge their wisdom to have foreseen the issues and problems America would face in dealing with a government of the people, by the people and for the people while charged with overseeing the mutual interests of all peoples and at the same time maintaining the rights and freedoms of all individuals. Their courage, wisdom and foresight exemplify the incredible strength and endurance of the *American Spirit.*

The American democratic process empowers individuals to explore, experiment, innovate, build and succeed. Government as the *necessary evil* cannot be denied, nor can the people of America be apathetic to the evils of those in power of government, which, will given the opportunity, will dampen the spirit of achievement and tarnish the *American Dream* - either by intention or by the nature of power and government.

> * Conventional wisdom is the statement and belief
> of an individual or group of individuals, currently
> notable, given specific occurrences in the
> community, the nation or the world. Their
> wisdom has not necessarily stood the test of time
> and reason of common sense.

The process of pursuing the *American Dream* uncovers the highest and best use of the abundant resources available. Government cannot attempt to protect and provide for every potential contingency in order to keep an individual from injury or undue suffering. All peoples must take personal responsibility to endure and overcome whatever challenging situation exists for them. For government to attempt to deny this freedom to any individual capable of being responsible, at whatever their ability, to do so is demeaning and imprisons the power of the human spirit. It is acknowledged that not all people have equal abilities and thus, any government program designed must encourage them to be all they can be. Individuals are enlivened by what they endure and overcome. It is God's way and natural for humans to pursue what is possible for them. They are empowered and become productive contributors to society, rather than a burden on society. Addressing local issues and problems of a community is not a matter for the federal government. It is a matter for every citizen in the community to recognize the needs of each unique individual and support them in choosing to be personally responsible and self-reliant over being dependent solely on government. This is a virtue from which American pride explodes.

The matters and issues that face America are complex, yet the founding truths and principles are the beacons upon which to focus for making these trying and difficult choices that lay before the American people. More taxing and more spending to seek solutions to the issues and problems may have seemed proper in the past, but it has now proven to be absolutely ineffective. It once worked when few distinct categories of people existed. Today, there are multiple categories of people who have created communities to serve them and their unique needs. No government program or bureaucracy is capable of caring for people they have no experience of living the daily life they live. We must take our knowledge, education, experience, and resources tempered with natural reason, common sense and with America's founding truths and principles as the guiding beacon to empower all people to be the best they can be.

Returning To Wisdom (1995)

When the political rhetoric, opinion polls, commentaries, talk shows, speeches and sound-bites fade away, one is left with personal thoughts and opinions on the state of affairs in America. The turbulent and chaotic times of the last thirty years opened the doors of equal opportunities for all Americans, yet left America fragmented and searching for answers to a multitude of special interest issues and problems. The value of the process will be recorded in history as the birth of a new era. An era of understanding and strengthening of the wisdom, truths, principles and values of liberty and freedom intended by America's Founders and promised by the Constitution and Bill of Rights.[82]

Instead of the selfish bantering, blaming and political positioning of special interests, Americans will return to the wisdom that made America the greatest nation on earth. In the process, the issues and problems that critically loom throughout the nation will become issues to be addressed by and resolved by local leaders and citizens in demonstration of true *American Spirit* and the *Faithful Majority*.

America's Founders absolutely knew, because of their personal

---

82   It is truly amazing to see the development of the Internet over the past twenty years and how multiple and unique communities of interest have exploded.

acquired knowledge and personal experiences, that an individual's spirit and mind could not be imprisoned. Natural reason and common sense always prevailed and government was a necessary evil for the purpose of addressing mutual interests of freedom and security. Thus the United States of America was formed under the Constitution of the United States and the Bill of Rights and all Americans are entitled to Life, Liberty and the pursuit of Happiness. Let us return to our heritage that has provided for and moved us forward in times past.

For the purpose of maintaining perspective, the reader should note that in the American revolutionary period, an individual's accomplishments, writing and speaking ability were viewed and judged critically by his immediate peers and the electorate. There was no mass media. The leaders could not be *dressed for success*, hire the best speech writer or be coached by the latest PR guru. America's Founders stood face to face with their peers. They had the opportunity to demonstrate true wisdom and leadership in face to face debates, town meetings and in newspapers, pamphlets and letters. They had to endure not only ridicule from broadsides and articles in newspapers written by others under an assumed name, but also from a distance through letters penned and delivered directly to them. In which, they were often judged closely by their peers and the electorate on their ability to deliver deliberate, focused, clear and concise thoughts on the current issues of the day. They did so without the use of speech writers, Teleprompters and without advertising with biased media sound-bites designed to enrage instead of encouraging.

Their prior accomplishments and status, their writings, speaking and debates heightened their strengths and weaknesses directly in the eyes of the electorate. Today's politicians are forced to access the mass media and are dependent upon sound-bite images, mud-slinging and delivering the empty promises of, "lower taxes, less government, more money to those who seek to forego their freedoms and an easy handout and special privileges for whomever or whatever group they are currently speaking to at the moment. Seldom are the true issues addressed. Educating the electorate does not happen in sound-bites.

Do we fault the politicians? Not completely, because they want to get elected and they must do what it takes to get elected.

Although we can fault them for the example they set for our children. Do we fault the media? Not completely, because their job is to report the news and they must do it in sound-bites that get attention and make an impact, without which they do not attract viewers that drive the advertisers to want to sell their products. The bottom line rules the media, as with any private enterprise. Do we fault the lobbyists? Not completely, because they are hired to represent a special interest that feels they have a legitimate concern, and those individuals of the special interests feel they must protect their interests. Do we fault the American people? Not completely, because most everyone has personal, family and community obligations and what time they have will always be precious. Remember, they are the *Faithful Majority.* They exhibit their faith in the American way by generally expecting things to be taken care of by their representatives.

Is it important to find fault or is it more important to just get the job done with the highest and best results, and with the least amount of suffering for the least number of people?

Some politicians would appreciate more time and the forums to demonstrate their wisdom and leadership, but if it takes more than a few seconds, few people really take the time to listen. So, the knowledgeable, wise and courageous politician gets lost in the sea of sound-bites. The media simply reacts to the wants of the people. Talk radio, talk television and on-line computer services are much more serving to these issues, but none have the ability to reach the masses when every major television and radio network is reporting the latest hot news flash in a sensationally engineered sound-bite.[83] Now there is the issue of fairness in media and whether or not the flood of talk shows is representative of America. This will be an issue debated for a long time. But the most important aspect of this issue is that Government should keep out.

The times in which we live today are more demanding, and information flows so abundantly that it is difficult for someone to truly capture an understanding and appreciation of an individual's wisdom and capacity to lead America through the coming years.

---

83 Obviously, the Internet's numerous social-media applications have changed all this in 2012. Yet, it still takes responsible citizens to take the time to read, think, understand and make decisions for themselves.

It is my hope that more Americans will take on the responsibility and decide for themselves. They will pursue a deeper understanding and appreciation of the founding wisdom of America and the type of leadership that is necessary to maintain and grow this great nation. While personality and proper education are an issue, character is vital. Also, it is my hope that current politicians and political candidates will return to the understanding that it is a privilege to serve and stand within the ranks of the rich heritage of America's Founders and all of those men and women of wisdom and common sense, who have served America proudly. It is not the duty of a politician to make the American people servants of the government.

The following selected writings and quotes were chosen because the content demonstrates the dynamic thought process of a few of the individuals actively engaged in founding and nurturing the growth of the United States.

The following writings, speeches and quotes refer primarily to "man". The author refuses to buy into the concept of being politically correct. The author believes and knows that the Founders, if alive today, would respect the rights of all humans, regardless of gender, race, creed, color, religion or political preference. To focus on such petty issues is a ruse to focus on what truly is important. It is the readers' responsibility to place the writings into historical and personal perspective, and respect and enjoy the value of the wisdom, truths and principles that have made America great.

The situations of a federal deficit, growing bureaucracies, congressional abuses and *tax and spend* abuses have all happened before, as witnessed by the following letters, speeches and writings by America's Founders and early American leaders. The task at hand for today's political leaders is not an easy task. Breaking from *Politics As Usual* demands a presence and wisdom to be admired and praised. This is why all Americans must come together in unity and cooperation.

The writings and printing of speeches by America's Founders and early leaders reveals the true nature of what it is to be an American.

The World According to Our Children
(1995)
~ Poem by Alan W. Goldsberry ~

Through our children's journey
  Of their birth,
We witness the awesome power of life.

Through our children's voice,
  We hear the world's
Melodic, angelic symphony.

Through our children's touch
  We feel the
Miracle and magic of life.

Through our children's eyes,
  The world's illusions are
Unveiled - the reality difficult to ignore.

Through our children's senses,
  The sights, sounds and fragrance of
Nature's wonders halt the chaos.

Through our children's questions,
  Our answers, filtered by their innocence,
Unmask our charades.

Through our children's struggle
  To understand,
We desire the world to be a better place.

Through our children's accomplishments,
  We anticipate
Their contribution to humanity.

Through our children's laughter,
  We rejoice and bless
All that makes them unique.

Through our children's heart,
    Love and peace for all humankind
Becomes a possibility.

Through our children's soul,
    The spirit of God provides a
Glimpse of the way life is meant to be.

PART SIX
From the Birth of America to Sustainable Greatness (1995)
A Collection of Quotes and Commentary

Declaration of Independence

Authored primarily by Thomas Jefferson and unanimously approved on July 4, 1776.

When in the Course of human events, it becomes necessary for one people to dissolve the political bands which have connected them with another, and to assume among the Powers of the earth, the separate and equal station to which the Laws of Nature and of Nature's God entitle them, a decent respect to the opinions of mankind requires that they should declare the causes which impel them to the separation.

We hold these truths to be self-evident, that all men are created equal, that they are endowed by their Creator with certain inalienable Rights, that among these are Life, Liberty and the pursuit of Happiness. That to secure these rights, Governments are instituted among Men, deriving their just powers, from the consent of the governed, That whenever any Form of Government becomes destructive to these ends, it is the Right of the People to alter or to abolish it, and to institute new Government, laying its foundation on such principles and organizing its powers in such form, as to them shall seem most likely to effect their Safety and Happiness. Prudence, indeed, will dictate that Governments long established should not be changed for light and transient causes; and accordingly all experience hath shown, that mankind are more disposed to suffer, while evils are sufferable, than to right themselves by abolishing the forms to which they are accustomed. But when a long train of abuses and usurpations, pursuing invariably the same Object evinces a design to reduce them under absolute Despotism, it is their right, it is their duty, to throw off such Government, and to provide new Guards for their future security. Such has been the patient sufferance of these Colonies; and such is now the necessity which contains them to alter their former Systems of Government.

> Author's Note: *...necessary...to dissolve the political bands ...Governments long established should not be changed for light and transient causes... mankind is more disposed to suffer, while evils are sufferable... it is their right, it is their duty ...and to provide new Guards for their future security... Such has been the patient sufferance...and now the necessity...to alter their Systems of Government.*

Jefferson knew that change was inevitable and he understood the nature of humanity. Changes were to be made, when necessary; yet not at the whims of an individual or minority of a political party. Humanity will put up with a lot of inconveniences, but at some point it is the right and the duty of humanity to secure a future and make changes. Today, the infrastructure of American government, the three branches of government must remain, but the Systems which *Politics As Usual* has put into place during the last sixty years desperately needs restructuring, in order to fit the changes that have taken place in the world.

America's Founders sought a peaceful resolution with England. As Paine wrote, *"Men of all ranks have embarked in the controversy; from different motives, and with various designs; but all have been ineffectual, and the period of debate is closed. Arms as the last resource decide the contest; the appeal was the choice of the King, and the Continent has accepted the challenge..."*

Americans today do not seek *arms as the last resource.* Americans today demand wisdom and common sense from their leaders to shape new Systems of government which support and inspire all Americans to accept their personal responsibility to seek out and secure their personal individual *Rights of Life, Liberty and the pursuit of Happiness.*

Constitution of the United States
(1787) & Bill of Rights (Preamble only)

We, the People of the United States, in Order to form a more perfect Union, establish Justice, insure domestic Tranquility, provide for the common defence, promote the general Welfare, and secure the Blessings of Liberty to ourselves and our Posterity, do ordain and establish this Constitution for the United States of America.

> Author's Note: *We, the People...* That includes all of us, folks. There is no one to blame but ourselves. We live in a nation that makes broad promises to all citizens and all citizens must accept the personal responsibility of making it happen.

Thomas Jefferson's First Inaugural Address (March 4, 1801)
(excerpts regarding the general activities of government)

...a wise and frugal government, which shall restrain men from injuring one another; which shall leave them otherwise free to regulate their own pursuits of industry and improvement, and shall not take from the mouth of labor the bread it has earned. This is the sum of good government, and this is necessary to close the circle of our felicities.

> Author's Note: How much more clearly does it have to be? Immense and incredible business, professional and career opportunities exist for every American. Personal improvement is a choice by each individual and no amount of money or government regulations are going to force everyone to do what they must individually do to make themselves a part of this new era.

...Equal and exact justice to all men, of whatever state or persuasion, religious or political; peace, commerce, and honest friendship, with all nations---entangling alliances with none; the support of the state governments in all their rights, as the most competent administrations for our domestic concerns and the surest bulwarks against anti-republican tendencies; the preservation of the general government in its whole constitutional vigor, as the sheet anchor of our peace at home and safety abroad; a jealous care of the right of election by the people---a mild and safe corrective of abuses which are lopped by the sword of the revolution where peaceable remedies are unprovided; absolute acquiescence in the decision of the majority---the vital principle of republics, from which there is no appeal but to force, the vital principle and immediate parent of despotism; a well-disciplined militia---our best reliance in peace and for the first moments of war, til regulars may relieve them; the supremacy of the civil over the military authority; economy in the public expense, that labor may be lightly burdened; the honest payment of debts and sacred preservation of the public faith; encouragement of agriculture, and of commerce as its handmaid; the diffusion of information and the arraignment of all abuses at the bar of public reason; freedom of religion; freedom of the press; freedom of person under the protection of the habeas corpus; and trial by juries impartially selected---these principles form the bright constellation which has gone before us, and guided our steps through an age of revolution and reformation. The wisdom of our sages and the blood of our heroes have been devoted to their attainment. They should be the creed or our political faith---the text of civil instruction---the touchstone by which to try the services of those we trust; **and should we wander from them in moments of error or alarm, let us hasten to retrace our steps and to regain the road which alone leads to peace, liberty, and safety...**

> Author's Note: And so our work begins and keeps going and going...

The American Experiment: On Going Questions & Continuous Improvement

Letter from Thomas Jefferson to David Hartley (1787)

I have no fear, but that the result of our experiment will be, that men may be trusted to govern themselves without a master. Could the contrary of this be proved, I should conclude, either there is no

God, or that he is a malevolent being.

Alexander Hamilton addressing of the Whiskey Rebellion (1794)

It has, from the first establishment of your present Constitution, been predicted, that every occasion of serious embarrassment which should occur in the affairs of the government, every misfortune which it should experience, whether produced from its own faults or mistakes, or from other causes, would be the signal of an attempt to overthrow it, or to lay the foundation of its overthrow, by defeating the exercise of constitutional and necessary authorities. The disturbances which have recently broken out in the western counties of Pennsylvania, furnish an occasion of this sort...

Virtuous and enlightened citizens of a new and happy country! ye could not be the dupes of artifices so detestable, of a scheme so fatal; ye cannot be insensible to the destructive consequences with which it would be pregnant; ye cannot but remember that the government is YOUR own work, that those who administer it are but your temporary agents; that you are called upon not to support their power, BUT YOUR OWN POWER. And you will not fail to do what your rights, your best interests, your character as a people, your security as members of society, conspire to demand you...

Author's Note: We cannot overthrow ourselves, but we can elect wise and reasonable leaders.

Passing the Test: America Has Been There Before

Thomas Jefferson's First Annual Message to Congress (December 8, 1801)

These views, however, of reducing our burdens, are formed on the expectation that a sensible, and at the same time a salutary reduction, may take place in our habitual expenditures. For this purpose those of the civil government, the army, and navy, will need revisal.

When we consider that this government is charged with the external and mutual relations only of these states; that the states themselves have principal care of our persons, our property, and our reputation, constituting the great field of human concerns, we may well doubt whether our organization is not too complicated, too expensive; whether offices and officers have not been multiplied unnecessarily, and sometimes injuriously to the service they were meant to promote. I will cause to be laid before you an essay toward a statement of those who, under public employment of various kinds, draw money from the treasury or from our citizens. Time has not permitted a perfect enumeration, the ramifications of office being too multiplied and remote to be completely traced in a first trial. Among those who are dependent on executive discretion, I have begun the reduction of what was deemed necessary...

...But the great mass of public offices is established by law, and, therefore, by law alone can be abolished. Should the legislature think it expedient to pass this roll in review, and try all its parts by the test of public utility, they may be assured of every aid and light which executive information can yield. Considering general tendency to multiply offices and dependencies, and to increase expense to the ultimate term of burden which the citizen can bear, it behoove us to avail ourselves of every occasion which present itself for taking off the surcharge; that it never may be seen here that, after leaving to labor the smallest portion of its earnings on which can subsist, government shall itself consume the residue of what it was instituted to guard.

In our care, too, of public contributions entrusted to our direction, it would be prudent to multiply barriers against this dissipation, by appropriating specific sums to every specific purpose susceptible of definition; by disallowing all applications of money varying from the appropriation in object, or transcending it in amount; by reducing the undefined field of contingencies, and thereby circumscribing discretionary powers over money; and by bringing back to a single department all accountabilities for money where the examination may be prompt, efficacious, and uniform...

Authors Note: It is time to heed to the wisdom of America's mentor regarding the designs of

government, its shortcomings and what our duties
are that we must do.

Thomas Jefferson's Second Inaugural Address (March 4, 1805)

...At home, fellow citizens, you best know whether we have done
well or ill. **The suppression of unnecessary offices, of useless
establishments and expenses, enabled us to discontinue our
internal taxes.** These covering our land with officers, and opening
our doors to their intrusions, had already begun that process of
domiciliary vexation which, once entered, is scarcely to be
restrained from reaching successively every article of produce and
property. If among these taxes some minor ones fell which had not
been inconvenient, it was because their amount would not have
paid the officers who collected them, and because, if they had any
merit, the state authorities might adopt them, instead of others less
approved.

...it may meet within the year all the expenses of the year,
**without encroaching on the rights of future generations, by
burdening them with the debts of the past.**

Andrew Jackson's Farewell Address (1837)

We have had our seasons of peace and of war, with all the evils
which precede or follow a state of hostility with powerful nations.
We encountered these trials with our Constitution yet in its infancy,
and under the disadvantages which a new untried Government
must always feel when it is called upon to put forth its whole
strength, without the lights of experience to guide it or the weight
of precedents to justify its measures. But we have passed
triumphantly through all these difficulties. Our Constitution is no
longer a doubtful experiment; and , at the end of nearly half a
century, we find that it has preserved unimpaired the liberties of
the people, secured the rights of property, and that our country has
improved and is flourishing beyond any former example in the
history of nations...

...Experience, the unerring test of all human undertakings has
shown the wisdom and foresight of those who formed it; and has

proved that in the union of these States there is a sure foundation for the brightest hopes of freedom and for the happiness of the people. At every hazard and by every sacrifice, this Union must be preserved.

The progress of the United States under our free and happy institutions has surpassed the most sanguine hopes of the founders of the Republic. Our growth has been rapid beyond all former example, in numbers, in wealth, in knowledge, and all the useful arts which contribute to the comforts and convenience of man; and from the earliest ages of history to the present day, there never have been thirteen millions of people associated together in one political body who enjoyed so much freedom and happiness as the people of these United States.

It is from within, among yourselves, from cupidity, from corruption, from disappointed ambition, and inordinate thirst for power, that factions will be formed and liberty endangered. It is against such designs, whatever disguise the actors may assume, that you have especially to guard yourselves. Providence has showered on this favored land blessings without number and has chosen you as the guardians of freedom to preserve it for the benefit of the human race. May He who holds in his hands the destinies of nations make you worthy of the favors He has bestowed and enabled you, with pure hearts and pure hands and sleepless vigilance, to guard and defend to the end of time the great charge He has committed to your keeping.

A Process That Works

Thomas Jefferson's quote regarding his Cabinet.

...presented an example of harmony in a cabinet of six persons, to which perhaps history has furnished no parallel. There never arose, during the whole time, an instance of an unpleasant thought or word between the members. We sometimes met under differences of opinion, but scarcely ever failed, by conversing and reasoning, so to modify each others' ideas, as to produce a unanimous result.

Political Duty

Thomas Jefferson commenting on this duty to America

"The whole of my life has been a war with my natural taste, feelings and wishes; domestic life and literary pursuits were my first and my latest inclinations—circumstances and not my desires led me to the path I have trod, and like a bow though long bent, which when unstrung flies back to its natural state, I resume with delight the character and pursuits for which nature designed me. The circumstances of our country, at my entrance into life, were such that every honest man felt himself compelled to take part, and to act up to the best of his abilities."

George Washington goes on to say:

"...Let me now take a more comprehensive view, and warn you in the most solemn manner against the baneful effects of the Spirit of Party, generally.

This Spirit, unfortunately, is inseparable from our nature, having its root in the strongest passions of human mind. - It exists under different shapes in all Governments, more or less stifled, controlled, or repressed; but, in those of the popular form, it is seen in its greatest rankness, and is truly their worst enemy.

The alternative domination of one faction over another, sharpened by the spirit of revenge, natural to party dissension, which in different ages and countries has perpetrated the most horrid enormities, is itself a frightful despotism. -But this leads at length to a more formal and permanent despotism. -The disorders and miseries, which result, gradually incline the minds of men to seek security and repose in the absolute power of an Individual; and sooner or later the chief of some prevailing faction, more able or more fortunate than his competitors, turns this disposition to the purposes of his own elevation, on the ruins of Public Liberty.

Without looking forward to an extremity of this kind, (which nevertheless ought not to be entirely out of sight), the common and continual mischief of the spirit of Party are sufficient to make it the interest and duty of a wise people to discourage and restrain it.

It serves always to distract the Public Councils, and enfeeble the Public administration. It agitates the community with ill-founded jealousies and false alarms, kindles the animosity of one part against another, and foments occasionally riot and insurrection. -It opens the door to foreign influence and corruption, which find a facilitated access to Government itself through the channels of party passions."...

Taxation Abuse

> *There is no art which one government sooner learns of another than that of draining money from the pockets of the people.* ~ Adam Smith ~

Thomas Jefferson's letter to Samuel Kercheval

If we run into such debts, as that we must be taxed in our meat and in our drink, in our necessaries and our comforts, in our labors and our amusements, for our callings and our creeds, as the people of England are, our people, like them, must come to labor sixteen hours in the twenty-four, give the earnings of fifteen of these to the government for their debts and daily expenses; and the sixteenth being insufficient to afford us bread, we must live, as they now do, on oatmeal and potatoes; have no time to think, no means of calling the mismanagers to account; but be glad to obtain subsistence by hiring ourselves to rivet their chains on the necks of our fellow-sufferers.

Andrew Jackson's Farewell Address (1837)

There is, perhaps no one of the powers conferred on the Federal Government so liable to abuse as the taxing power. The most productive and convenient sources of revenue were necessarily given to it, that it might be able to perform the important duties imposed upon it; and the taxes which it lays upon commerce being concealed from the real payer in the price of the article, they do not so readily attract the attention of the people as smaller sums demanded from them directly by the tax gatherer. But the tax imposed on goods enhances by so much the price of the commodity to the consumer; and, as many of these duties are imposed on articles of necessity which are daily used by the great body of the people, the money raised by these imposts is drawn from their pockets. Congress has no right, under the Constitution to take money from the people unless it is required to execute some one of the specific powers entrusted to the Government; and if they raise more than is necessary for such purposes, it is an abuse of the power of taxation and unjust and oppressive. It may, indeed, happen that the revenue will sometimes exceed the amount anticipated when the taxes were laid. When, however, this is ascertained, it is easy to reduce them; and, in such a case, it is unquestionably the duty of the Government to reduce them, for no circumstances can justify it in assuming a power not given to it by the Constitution nor in taking away the money of the people when it is not needed for legitimate wants of the Government.

Plain as these principles appear to be, you will yet find that there is a constant effort to induce the General Government to go beyond the limits of its taxing power and to impose unnecessary burdens upon the people. Many powerful interests are continually at work at procure heavy duties on commerce to swell the revenue beyond the real necessities of the public service; and the country has already felt the injurious effects of their combined influence.

...efforts will be made to seduce and mislead the citizens of the several States by holding out to them the deceitful prospect of benefits...

The Power of the People

Thomas Jefferson's letter to Colonel William S. Smith

God forbid we should ever be 20 years without such a rebellion...What country can preserve its liberties if its rulers are not warned from time to time that this people preserve the spirit of resistance? ...The tree of liberty must be refreshed from time to time with the blood of patriots and tyrants. It is its natural manure.

George Bancroft (1835)

The spirit, which is the guide to truth, is the gracious gift to each member of the human family.

If it be true, that the gifts of mind and heart are universally diffused, if the sentiment of truth, justice, love and beauty exists in every one, then it follows, as a necessary consequence, that the common judgment in taste, politics, and religion, is the highest authority on earth, and the nearest possible approach to an infallible decision. From the consideration of the individual powers I turn to the action of the human mind in masses.

Self Reliance by Ralph Waldo Emerson

"If our young men miscarry in their first enterprises they lose all heart. If the young merchant fails, men say he is ruined. If the finest genius studies at one of our colleges, and is not installed in an office within one year afterwards, in the cities or suburbs of Boston or New York, it seems to his friends and to himself that he is right in being disheartened and in complaining the rest of his life. A sturdy lad from New Hampshire or Vermont, who in turn tries all the professions, who teams it, farms it, peddles, keeps a school, preaches, edits a newspaper, goes to Congress, buys a township, and so forth, in successive years, and always like a cat falls on his feet, is worth a hundred of these city dolls. He walks abreast with his days and feels no shame in not "studying a profession," for he does not postpone his life, but lives already. He has not one chance, but a hundred chances."

America the Great and Its Destiny to Remain Great

George Bancroft (1835)

Wherever you see men clustering together to form a party, you may be sure that however much error may be there, truth is there also. Apply this principle boldly; for it contains a lesson of candor, and a voice of encouragement. There never was a school of philosophy, nor a clan in the realm of opinion, but carried along with it some important truth. And therefore every sect that has ever flourished has benefited Humanity; for the errors of a sect pass away and are forgotten; its truths are received into the common inheritance. To know the seminal thought of every prophet and leader of a sect, is to gather all the wisdom of mankind...

In like manner the best government rests on the people and not on the few, on persons and not on property, on the free development of public opinion and not on authority; because the munificent Author of our being has conferred the gifts of mind upon every member of the human race without distinction or outward circumstances. Whatever of other possessions may be engrossed, mind asserts its own independence.

...A government of equal rights must, therefore, rest upon mind; not wealth, not brute force, the sum of the moral intelligence of the community should rule the State...

...The public happiness is the true object of legislation, and can be secured only by the masses of mankind themselves awakening to the knowledge and the care of their own interests...

...The world can advance only through the culture of the moral and intellectual powers of the people. To accomplish this end by means of the people themselves, is the highest purpose of government.

...The duty of America is to secure the culture and the happiness of the masses by their reliance on themselves.

Abraham Lincoln (February 11, 1859)
Lecture on "Discoveries and Inventions", to a group of young people in Jacksonville,   Illinois.

"The great difference between Young America and Old Fogy, is the result of "Discoveries, Inventions, and Improvements." These in turn, are the result of "observation, reflection and experiment." For instance, it is quite certain that ever since water has been boiled in covered vessels, men have seen the lids of the vessels rise and fall a little, with a sort of fluttering motion, by force of the steam; but so long as this was not specially observed, and reflected and experimented upon, it came to nothing. At length however, after many thousand years, some man observes this long-known effect of hot water lifting a pot-lid, and begins a train of reflection upon it. he says "Why, to be sure the force that lifts the pot-lid, will lift any thing else, which is no heavier than the pot-lid." "And, as man has much hard lifting to do, can not this hot-water power be made to help him?" He has become a little excited on the subject, and he fancies he hears a voice answering "Try me". He does try it; and the "observation, reflection, and trial" gives to the world the control of that tremendous, and now well known agent, called steam-power. This is not the actual history in detail, but the general principle."

"But was this first inventor of the application of steam, wiser or more ingenious than those who had gone before him? Not at all. Had he not learned much of them, he never would have succeeded--probably, never would have thought of making the attempt. To be fruitful in invention, it is indispensable to have a habit of observation and reflection; and this habit, our steam friend acquired, no doubt, from those who, to him, were old fogies. But for the difference in habit of observation, why did yankees, almost instantly, discover gold in California, which had been trodden upon, and overlooked by Indians and Mexicans, for centuries? Goldmines are not the only mines overlooked in the same way. There are more mines above the Earth's surface than below it. All nature--the whole world, material, moral, and intellectual,--is a mine;"

The Future Awaits Our Actions Today and Other Ideas to Think About

The future is happening today. People like you are making things happen in all realms and facets of society, business, community and governments. Old beliefs of the way to do something to get things done and make things happen are being changed by common folks, just like you and I and America's Founders. These following book excerpts have been provided to inspire those who have yet to get inspired, quicken the pace of those already inspired into taking actions and to temper where, and if, temperance may be needed. While many of the concepts, thoughts and ideas have been stated previously, these passages restate it in a variety of ways. So, I share these with the reader in hopes they will find a point or additional points of reference to relate to. I also highly recommend reading the books and then join in the process of democratic thinking and get into the action. It is time to re-educate ourselves and bring back the voice of reason and plain ole' common sense.

Much is happening in the world. There can be no question that change is happening and that opportunities exist. Most of us believe that our future is full of excitement and a few individuals stand as the perennial doomsayers. Yet, the future is unknown and we must proceed. Enterprise and commerce rules the future and we must deal with the many social issues in the process of personal and business growth and development. It is not the duty of government to address these issues, unless they can be efficient and effective in doing so.

James Patterson & Peter Kim, <u>The Second American Revolution</u>

To read the papers, to watch the nightly news, you'd think that Americans had given up on their country. You'd think citizens had lost faith in their government.

We didn't find cynicism. We didn't find hopelessness. We found a determination to find creative solutions.

Americans are ready to fix America.

THE TIME IS NOW

We can wait a year or two. Maybe three. But not much more. The problems are mounting. The crises are multiplying. The nation is crumbling. And we stand by and watch.

We've identified the problems.

We've chosen our solutions.

It's time to stop waiting.

Now it's time to act.

Now it's time to fix America.

William Greider, <u>Who will tell the People</u>

Rehabilitating democracy will require citizens to devote themselves first to challenging status quo, disrupting the existing contours of power and opening the way for renewal. The ultimate task, however is even more difficult than that: building something new that creates the institutional basis for politics as a shared experience. The search for democratic meaning is necessarily a path of hard conflict, but the distant horizon is reconciliation. Americans coming to terms with themselves - that is the high purpose politics was meant to serve.

This renewal, if it occurs, will not come from books. A democratic insurgency does not begin with ideas, as intellectuals presume, or even with great political leaders who seize the moment. It originates among the ordinary people who find the will to engage themselves with their surrounding reality and to question the conflict between what they are told and what they see and experience...

The American beacon helped to teach people everywhere to aspire to self-realization and to rebel against powerlessness. Now, it seems, the former students must re-educate Americans in the meaning of their own faith. Perhaps that is when the American movement will begin: when Americans find the courage to speak honestly again in the language of democracy.

Rush Limbaugh, <u>See I Told You So</u>

How do we fight back? Well, we've got to begin by having an honest and open debate about the problem - without name-calling and *ad hominem* attacks. We've got to stop pretending that everything's okay and stop lying to ourselves by saying that there's nothing that can be done to change people's behavior. It's time to start championing old-fashioned virtues like fidelity, chastity, sobriety, self-restraint, self-discipline and self-reliance, and responsibility. Is that so unthinkable? Is that too much to ask?

John Naisbitt & Patricia Aburdene, <u>Megatrends 2000</u>

Across the world, there is now a clear shift of emphasis to the individual from class or group (poor blacks, unwed mothers). In the past it has been: We are going to do this, or should do that, for *them*. Now the focus is shifting to the individual. Surely what works best is a tailored program to match individual strengths and needs, to have government in concert with the private sector respond to each individual, not to classes and groups and categories.

The basic shift is from central government to individual empowerment:

From public housing to homeownership

From national health service to private options

From government regulation to market mechanisms

From welfare to workfare

From collectivism to individualism

From government monopoly to competitive enterprise

From state industries to privatized companies

From government Social Security plans to private insurance and investment

From tax burdens to tax reductions

Author's Note: So why is Politics As Usual so out of step?

Paul Zane Pilzer, Unlimited Wealth

"Of all the enormous technological gains we have witnessed in recent years, advances in information-processing technology have been the most impressive. In fact, the science of information processing has reached a state of critical mass-breakthroughs in today's computers come directly from yesterday's breakthroughs, computer programs write other programs, and computers actually design computers that design other computers. The multiplier effect of information-processing technology has caused an explosive advance, which has led to an ever-growing backlog of unimplemented resource technology. As a result, despite the meteoric rise in GNP over the past decade, we have barely scratched the surface of what is currently possible and what is about to become possible."

Ken Dychtwald, Ph.D., <u>Age Wave</u>

All around us, millions of ordinary aging Americans have begun to break free of the traditional expectations of age to shape new and rewarding cyclic lives for themselves.

As America ages (meaning its people), not only will we relate most closely with those blood and marital relatives with whom we feel the greatest affinity, but we will find in our networks of close friends, workmates, and neighbors the love, support, and companionship that our relatives cannot provide.

Robert Muller, <u>New Genesis</u>

...humanity is undergoing a deep evolutionary change and will develop new means and perceptions which will help it survive and find a harmonious relation with its planet and with its own individuals.

...we must restor optimism and continue to sharpen our inborn instincts for life, for the positive, for self-preservation, for survival and human fulfillment at ever higher levels of consciousness. We must conquer the duality, the somber, the bad, the negative, the suicidal. These all contain dangerous self-feeding processes of destruction. We must turn instead to the mysterious self-generating powers of hope, creative thinking, love, life affirmation and faith as they were taught to us by Chirst and by all great religious leaders.

The greatest freedom of the human being is his choice to believe in life and in himself and thus to be fully part of the eternal stream of creation and evolution.

It is the fundamental task of education to teach all new members of the human family to give optimistic guidance to their miraculous bodies, minds, hearts and souls in the complexity of our stupendous reality.

Interdependence, globality and a total view of our planet and the environment are now facts of life.

Peter F. Drucker, <u>Innovation and Entrepreneurship</u>

...We know that "revolution" is not achievement and the new

dawn. It results from senile decay, from the bankruptcy of ideas and institutions, from failure or self-renewal.

And yet we also know that theories, values, and all the artifacts of human minds and human hands do age and rigidify, becoming obsolete, becoming "afflictions."

Innovation and entrepreneurship are thus needed in society as much as in the economy, in public-service institutions as much as in businesses. It is precisely because innovation and entrepreneurship are not "root and branch" but "one step at a time," a product here, a policy there, a public service yonder; because they are not planned but focused on this opportunity and that need; because they are tentative and will disappear if they do not produce the expected and needed results; because, in other words, they are pragmatic rather than dogmatic and modest rather than grandiose-that they promise to keep any society, economy, industry, public service, or business flexible and self-renewing. They achieve what (Thomas) Jefferson hoped to achieve through revolution in every generation, and they do without bloodshed, civil war, or concentration camps, without economic catastrophe, but with purpose, with direction, and under control.

What we need is an entrepreneurial society in which innovation and entrepreneurship are normal, steady, and continuous.

David Osborne and Ted Gaebler, Reinventing Government

...Our governments are in deep trouble today. In government after government and public system after public system, reinvention is the only option left. But the lack of a vision - a new paradigm - holds us back.

Yet there is hope. Slowly, quietly, far from the public spotlight, new kinds of public institutions are emerging. They are lean, decentralized, and innovative. They are flexible, adaptable, quick to learn new ways when conditions change. They use competition, customer choice, and other nonbureaucratic mechanisms to get things done as creatively and effectively as possible. And they are our future.

Governor Pete Wilson of California, 1991 Inaugural address:

We will not suffer the future. We will shape it. We will not simply grow. We will manage our growth. We will not passively experience change. We will make change. But to shape our future, we need a new vision of government.

John Naisbitt, <u>Global Paradox</u>

Politicians and political activity around the globe are being scrutinized, and where respect for standards of decency and ethical conduct are found wanting, the public is demanding retribution.

"...Revelations of corruption...violations...have become daily media fare. Flashed around the globe in a matter of seconds, information about each new atrocity fuels citizen outrage and escalates demands for redress.

...everyone will have to play by a new set of rules.

In the 21st century, citizens of the global community will be much less tolerant of perceived injustice in any form. This is certainly proving to be the case in the area of human rights.

When the onus is on the individual, individuals will reach decisions based on the same ethical standards they live by.

A revolutionary confluence of technological change has set the stage for a new environment that will empower individuals as never before.

George Gilder, <u>Microcosm</u>

The new technologies of the microcosm - artificial intelligence, silicon compilation, and parallel processing - all favor entrepreneurs and small companies. All three allow entrepreneurs to use the power of knowledge to economize on capital and enhance its efficiency: mixing sand and ideas to generate new wealth and power for men and women anywhere in the world.

Howard Rheingold, The Virtual Community

The technology that makes virtual communities possible has the potential to bring enormous leverage to ordinary citizens at relatively little cost - intellectual leverage, social leverage, commercial leverage, and most important, political leverage. But the technology will not in itself fulfill that potential; this latent technical power must be used intelligently and deliberately by an informed population. More people must learn about that leverage and learn how to use it, while we still have the freedom to do so if it is to live up to its potential.

...If a government is to rule according to the consent of the governed, the effectiveness of that government is heavily influenced by how much the governed know about the issues that affect them.

...The late 1990's may eventually be seen in retrospect as a narrow window of historical opportunity, when people either acted or failed to act effectively to regain control over communications technologies. Armed with knowledge, guided by a clear, human-centered vision, governed by a commitment to civil discourse, we the citizens hold the key levers at a pivotal time. What happens is largely up to us.

Harry S. Dent, The Great Boom Ahead

What we will be seeing in the future is the emergence of the corporate society - where large and small corporate networks become the basic social and community unit. Such diverse structures will combine large and small business and a full range of job opportunities. They will often be dispersed with central management and professional units in the big cities. But many sales and customer service units will be spread throughout the world. And many frontline-oriented staff consulting units will be located out in small towns and cities where the worker prefers to live. All of these segments will be connected by a common information system that keeps everyone in touch with everyone else. It will continually update everyone on what everyone else is doing - in real time. Obviously that means communication is instantaneous and synchronous. More important, it helps solidify a common overall mission and culture with dispersed units having the freedom to

161

develop in the localized cultures they need for their customers. Many more people will work in their homes part-time and full-time. Many other departments will be located in neighborhoods where people can be close to each other for work and social reasons with a minimum of commuting time and costs.

Alvin Toffler, Power Shift

...The use of violence as a source of power will not soon disappear. Students and protestors will still be shot in plazas around the world. Armies will still rumble across borders. Governments will still apply force when they imagine it serves their purposes. The state will never give up the gun.

Similarly, the control of immense wealth, whether by private individuals or public officials, will continue to confer enormous power on them. Wealth will continue to be an awesome tool of power.

Nevertheless, despite exceptions and unevenness, contradictions and confusions, we are witnessing one of the most important changes in the history of power.

For it is now indisputable that knowledge, the source of the highest-quality power of all, is gaining importance with every fleeting nanosecond.

The most important powershift of all, therefore, is not from one person, party, institution, or nation to another. It is the hidden shift in the relationships between violence, wealth, and knowledge as societies speed toward their collision with tomorrow.

This is the dangerous, exhilarating secret of the Powershift Era.

Milton & Rose Friedman, Free To Choose

Fortunately, we are waking up. We are again recognizing the dangers of an overgoverned society, coming to understand that good objectives can be perverted by bad means, that reliance on the freedom of people to control their own lives in accordance with their own values is the surest way to achieve the full potential of a great society.

Fortunately, also, we are as a people still free to choose which way we should go - whether to continue along the road we have been following to ever bigger government, or to call a halt and change direction.

Tom Peters, <u>Thriving On Chaos</u>

Moaning about bureaucracy is a time-honored management prerogative. Now, however, bureaucracy is beyond moaning about; it is a block to survival. <u>The campaigns against bureaucracy must become strategic priorities of the first order.</u> p. 377

Conclusion (1995)

America's government: of the people, by the people and for the people. That's us, folks. The reality of our past apathy and hopes in false-securities can no longer be denied. A few leaders will stand and inspire the *Faithful Majority*. I hope those leaders are simply awaiting confirmation that the wave of the *Faithful Majority* is moving towards shore.

America has no shortage of knowledge, information or experience. As a whole nation, we have not used much of our true *American Spirit* or much of our wisdom and common sense over the last couple of decades. There are many we can find to blame, but the many includes us all. What I see developing is a movement by the majority to bring together in a powerful combination the best of the thoughts and disciplines of the farmer/naturalist; the industrialist/capitalists; the compassion of the philanthropist and the socialist; and the excitement and dreams of the innovator/producer. We know we cannot control nature and we must not abuse nature. We cannot control the outcomes of our actions, but we can be responsible for the results of our actions and make changes, as needed. What we know of our minds and the lessons we have learned of the differences individuals have made in the world, we know our limits and we know where to put forth our efforts to achieve the impossible.

While the details of our decisions and actions as a nation remain uncertain, no one can deny *the American Spirit, the Human Spirit* to achieve and be the best it can be. It is an exciting period in the evolution of humanity. We have do have choices. That must be remembered. Choice must always be available. As I have heard in reference to hurricanes, people must evacuate from an approaching hurricane when the sun is shining. Likewise we must make changes while the times are good. If we wait until times are not so good and extremely challenging for many, the politicians will use *Politics As Usual* as a means to expand their influence on the American people by growing government through punishing regulation and taxes to enrich themselves. Our future awaits us. Our present demands the best of us.

APPENDIX

Framing Common Sense and the Faithful Majority (2012)

It is now only a few months before the 2012 Presidential elections. Great moments lay ahead for America. Many decisions must be made and the People will continually have a choice to maintain a sense of unity and collaborative participation or choose to be selfish to their own needs. This nation was born in the Spirit of collaborative participation. It is time to remember and renew all that we are as the American People to once again establish a government of the People, by the People and for the People – and, to remain vigilant, accountable and responsible for our thoughts, actions and comments. May our progeny bless and hold us in as high regard as we do the Founders of this great nation.

The following XY graph frames the progress of reason and common sense. A more detailed graph follows the first graph.

This graph can be used life a roadmap, as a simple means to determine where you are and where others are relative to one's thoughts, comments, behaviors and actions.

"The steady character of our countrymen is a rock to which we may safely moor." ~ Thomas Jefferson (1801) ~

- The **Community of Differences** represents those individuals whose opinions are generally not well thought-out for themselves. They seldom listen to engage in a discourse and are more likely to parrot sound-bites that support their selfish concerns and they are ready to be on the attack for anyone who has a different opinion. Their character and temperament can be for good or bad.

"The uniform tenor of a man's life furnishes better evidence of what he has said or done on any particular occasion than the word of an enemy, and of an enemy too who shows that he prefers the use of falsehoods which suit him to truths which do not." ~ Thomas Jefferson (1803) ~

- The **Community of Discourse** represents those individuals who allow for the differences of opinions and seek to engage with a sense of greater good being realized by their collaborative attitude and participation with others.

"In every country where man is free to think and to speak, differences of opinion will arise from difference of perception, and the imperfection of reason; but these differences when permitted, as in this happy country, to purify themselves by free discussion, are but as passing clouds overspreading our land transiently and leaving our horizon more bright and serene." ~ Thomas Jefferson (1801) ~

"I tolerate with the utmost latitude the right of others to differ from me in opinion without imputing to them criminality." ~ Thomas Jefferson (1804) ~

- The **Community of Special Interests** represents those individuals gather together with like-minded individuals. The groups that band together will have a temperament and character that represents each individual. As with individual people who reside in the Community of Differences, a group can be designed for good causes or bad.

"In every free and deliberating society, there must, from the nature of man, be opposite parties, and violent dissensions and discords; and one of these, for the most part, must prevail over the other for a longer or shorter time." ~ Thomas Jefferson (1798) ~

"To me... it appears that there have been differences of opinion and party differences, from the first

establishment of government to the present day, and on the same question which now divides our own country; that these will continue through all future time; that every one takes his side in favor of the many, or of the few, according to his constitution, and the circumstances in which he is placed... that as we judge between the those among us whose names may happen to be remembered for awhile, the next generations will judge favorably or unfavorably according to the complexion of individual minds and the side they shall themselves have taken; that nothing new can be added to what has been said by others and will be said in every age in support of the conflicting opinions on government; and that wisdom and duty dictate an humble resignation to the verdict of our future peers."
~ Thomas Jefferson (1813) ~

"Wherever there are men, there will be parties; and wherever there are free men they will make themselves heard. Those of firm health and spirits are unwilling to cede more of their liberty than is necessary to preserve order; those of feeble constitutions will wish to see one strong arm able to protect them from the many. These are the Whigs and Tories of nature. These mutual jealousies produce mutual security; and while the laws shall be obeyed, all will be safe. He alone is your enemy who disobeys them." ~ Thomas Jefferson (1801) ~

- The **Community of Leadership** represents those individuals who have been tested and proven of strong character and authentic leadership by their actions and results more than their words. Authentic leadership is thinking and acting on what is true at the core of the leader and the leader will think and act upon what is true and best for others.

"As the Creator has made no two faces alike, so no two minds, and probably no two creeds." ~ Thomas Jefferson (1821) ~

"The man who loves his country on its own account, and not merely for its trappings of interest or power, can never be divorced from it, can never refuse to come forward when he finds that she is engaged in dangers which he has the means of warding off." ~ Thomas Jefferson (1797) ~

"It is a blessing... that our people are reasonable; that they are kept so well informed of the state of things as to judge for themselves, to see the true sources of their difficulties, and to maintain their confidence undiminished in the wisdom and integrity of their functionaries." ~ Thomas Jefferson (1810) ~

"Time indeed changes manners and notions, and so far we must expect institutions to bend to them. But time produces also corruption of principles, and against this it is the duty of good citizens to be ever on the watch, and if the gangrene is to prevail at last, let the day be kept off as long as possible." ~ Thomas Jefferson (1821) ~

"We are to guard against ourselves; not against ourselves as we are, but as we may be; for who can imagine what we may become under circumstances not now imaginable?" ~ Thomas Jefferson (1822) ~

Download these graphs and more at:

http://zfactorgroup.com/downloads/

POLITICAL ACTION

Community of
Special Interests

Community of
Leadership

COMPLEXITY

Community of
Differences

Community of
Discourse

COLLABORATIVE PARTICIPATION

The Faithful Majority

Reveal and Release Untapped Potential for Unity and Collaborative Participation

We have no interests nor passions different from those of our fellow citizens. We have the same object: the success of representative government. Nor are we acting for ourselves alone, but for the whole human race... our experiment is to show whether man can be trusted with self-government. The eyes of suffering humanity are fixed on us... and on such a theatre, for such a cause, we must suppress all smaller passions and local considerations. ~ Thomas Jefferson (1802) ~

POLITICAL ACTION

Community of Special Interests

- Cause driven by self interests.
- Selfish beliefs and agenda put into actions.
- Political Action Committees. Interests contrary to the rights of others.
- Persuade others to change behaviors.
- Cooperative if serves their purpose.
- Rigid mindset. Willing to engage in direct confrontation for beliefs and values.
- Will blame, ridicule and spin the facts to fit their selfish agenda.
- Special interests drive political division. Faction versus faction.
- All about compromise—no collaboration.

Community of Leadership

- Influential with a sense of significance. Experienced, character and values tested.
- Sense of service above self interests. Interests for the whole community.
- Duty becomes a sense of calling to destiny.
- Focused on making a sustainable difference.
- Inclusive with clear vision, mission, goals.
- Collaborative with purpose to create new possibilities. Willing to cross party lines and make the tough decisions for the better good of all.
- Practical understanding with common sense.
- Coalition based upon the principles of justice and the general good.

COMPLEXITY

Community of Differences

- Either/Or thinking (right or wrong).
- Passionate with a selfish purpose.
- Self-centered (believe like me). Limited capacity to listen to other ideas or options.
- Beliefs driven by limited knowledge and experience (views pieces of the whole).
- Opinionated—repeats media-sound-bites and special interests messages.
- Dissension and distrusting of any different point of views—no matter the source.

Community of Discourse

- Both/And thinking.
- Compassionate seeking understanding.
- Passionate with a meaningful purpose—bigger than them. Emerging leadership.
- Strong values with deep relationships.
- Community building with other centers of influence.
- Willing to question beliefs with active listening focused on the whole and common good for all.
- Cooperative with desire to seek understanding.
- Focus in on others, not about themselves.

COLLABORATIVE PARTICIPATION

Download these graphs and more at:

http://zfactorgroup.com/downloads/